Discovering

ONTARIO'S

WINE

COUNTRY

· Discovering ·

ONTARIO'S

W·I·N·E

COUNTRY

Linda Bramble & Shari Darling

Stoddart

A BOSTON MILLS PRESS BOOK

Canadian Cataloguing in Publication Data

Bramble, Linda
    Discovering Ontario's wine country

Includes bibliographical references.
ISBN 1-55046-054-4

1. Wineries – Ontario – Guidebooks.   2. Wine and
wine making – Ontario.   I. Darling, Shari.
II. Title.

TP559.C2B73 1992   663'.2'09713   C92-093911-2

First published in 1992 by
Stoddart Publishing Co. Limited
34 Lesmill Road
Toronto, Canada
M3B 2T6

A BOSTON MILLS PRESS BOOK
The Boston Mills Press
132 Main Street
Erin, Ontario
N0B 1T0

Winners of the
Heritage Canada
Communications Award

American Association
for State and Local History
Award Winner

Edited by Noel Hudson
Design by Mary Firth
Typography by Justified Type, Guelph

The publisher gratefully acknowledges
the support of The Canada Council, Ontario
Arts Council and Ontario Publishing Centre
in the development of writing and publishing
in Canada.

Printed in Hong Kong
By Book Art Inc., Toronto

Contents

Foreword
by Tony Aspler

E very wine book is an odyssey, a journey of the mind and the senses to explore humankind's second most basic instinct: the urge to make wine from cultivated grapes. This compulsion is as natural and inevitable as the cycle of the seasons and we are the more civilized for it.

Discovering Ontario's Wine Country invites you to travel on three journeys: the literal and picturesque one that will take you along the province's wine route, past vineyards and farms, orchards and crushing facilities; the viticultural one that explains how Ontario wines are made, the grape varieties used and the techniques employed; and finally, the historical-geographical and geological road that explains the factors that make Ontario wines taste the way they do. The journey is enlightening and — just as good wine should be — refreshing and stimulating.

Every established wine-growing region has its own special characteristics that give its wines unique and readily identifiable taste profiles. It took the vintners of Bordeaux, Burgundy and the Rhineland centuries to perfect the great clarets, Chardonnays, Pinot Noirs and Rieslings we know today.

Cave Spring Cellars' new vineyards at the foot
of the Niagara escarpment

Although Ontario's wine industry can document itself back to 1811 (when Johann Schiller made wine from domesticated wild grapes that grew along the Credit River west of Toronto), it only began to deliver products of genuine quality in the late 1970s, when a few adventurous farmers planted the noble European varieties against the conventional wisdom of the day. After less than two decades, Ontario Rieslings and Chardonnays are now challenging their European models in quality and price, and they're developing a distinct, indigenous flavour that the world will one day call the Ontario style. With such progress, just think what will be possible in another decade!

Those who are familiar with the wines of Ontario's producers will find this volume a comprehensive and indispensable guide to the region. Those who have yet to discover Ontario wines are in for a surprise that borders on revelation. And when you have travelled these roads you will thank Linda Bramble and Shari Darling for sharing with you their knowledge, their observations and their passion for the wines that grow in our own backyard.

T.A.
Toronto
March 1992

Introduction

T here has never been a more exciting time to discover Ontario's wine country. The countryside is beautiful, the wines are delicious, and the wineries' touring facilities are primed and ready.

Ontario's wine country is located within the remarkable Carolinian zone. This exceptionally mild climatic corridor of land, lying roughly south of Highway 401 from Toronto to Windsor, is similar in climate and habitat to the American Carolinas. Often called Eastern Canada's "banana belt," it is a national treasure, containing more rare, threatened and endangered plants and animals than any other place in Canada. Travelling its country roads is an inspiring adventure. And travelling through Ontario's wine country can be a wine-lover's dream.

Vidal grapes (above)

Ontario's wines are not what they used to be, thanks to a new generation of committed Canadians. These winemakers, growers, viticulturalists, scientists and investors are enthusiastic entrepreneurs whose vision is to produce world-class Ontario wines.

Unlike wines of the Old World, where districts determine style (Burgundy, Beaujolais, Mosel, etc.), Ontario's wines reflect the style of the winemaker. Since our winemakers come from or were educated in many different acclaimed wine regions, our wines reflect their multicultural origins. Not slaves to one tradition, but hosts to many, Ontario wines have become wines of the world.

To demonstrate their confidence in their vision, Ontario's winemakers have created comfortable tasting rooms, informative tours, and special events to welcome visitors.

In our busy lives today, it is easy to lose awareness of the products we consume, but wine touring offers a splendid opportunity for connection, for meeting the winemaker and others whose vision has produced the wines we savour. Enjoy your journey. Cheers!

A Brief History

*Wine brings to light the hidden secrets of the soul, gives being to our
hopes, bids the coward flight, drives dull care away, and teaches
new means for the accomplishment of our wishes.*
Horace, *Epistles, I.C.*, 5 B.C.

The most noble grapes in the world for making table wine come from
a European species called *Vitis vinifera*. Vines that grow naturally in
North America come from the classifications *Vitis riparia* and *Vitis labrusca*.
These native species were used for many years in Canadian winemaking
because the superior but more tender vinifera grapes could not survive our
winters. But through advancements in viticulture and technology, those noble
Old World varieties are now being grown in Ontario's own vineyards. Varieties
of vinifera number in the thousands, but probably no more than 50 concern
wine-lovers, and 46 of those now grow in Ontario.

Those who think that the phrase "Canadian wine" is an oxymoron are
uninformed. Things have changed rapidly in the Canadian wine industry;
there have been more changes in the past 20 years than in all its previous
history.

Ontario has been the centre of the Canadian wine industry since commercial production began in the 1850s. Winemaking in Ontario is currently
enjoying a renaissance far exceeding its own legacy. To appreciate that legacy,
and the accomplishments of the province's winemakers and viticulturalists,
we must take a brief look at the history of commercial winemaking in Ontario.

Sorting experimental root stock

Preparing the vineyards with a horse-drawn plough

HISTORY

Native grapes were found growing in Canada by the Viking explorers. These winter-hardy grapes (riparia and labrusca) were too "foxy" and unpleasant to produce fine table wines. They were, however, well suited to sherries and ports.

By the end of the 1800s thousands of acres of North American grapes were in production. But the sugar content of these grapes was so low that large quantities of sugar had to be added just prior to fermentation to increase the potential for producing alcohol. In many cases, alcohol was added directly, and in some of the early wines an alcohol content of 35 percent was reached.

In the early 1870s there was pressure for temperance reform, but not until the First World War, when alcohol was needed for the war effort, was public consumption prohibited.

The Ontario Temperance Act of 1916 made it illegal to sell liquor but not to manufacture it. A modification of the bill allowed manufacturers who held permits from the Board of License Commissioners to sell wines made from Ontario grapes. These licenses were handed out like cards at a poker table, and between 1917 and 1927, fifty-seven such licenses were issued. Just about anyone with room in his basement, store or pig shed became a licensed winemaker.

Ironically, prohibition would turn out to be the single largest contributing factor to the increase in wine production levels and in turning Canadians into a nation of wine drinkers.

Prohibition began in the U.S. in 1920 and gave new meaning to the terms free enterprise and free trade. With no laws to regulate quality, hygiene,

11

Modern mechanical harvesting

The harvest

pricing or distribution, the unscrupulous flourished. Many winemakers thought nothing of squeezing every grape until its pips squeaked, then adding water to stretch production even further. Only traces of colour remained, so winemakers added coal tar or vegetable dyes. Taste was not a factor in their winemaking equation.

After 11 years prohibition was unceremoniously repealed. In its place, provincial governments legislated strict controls over an industry gone amok. In 1927 the Liquor Control Board of Ontario (LCBO) was created to price, distribute and sell all liquor and wine in the province. In 1928 they also assumed quality control.

In the difficult 1930s the larger wineries were encouraged by the government to buy out the smaller ones, and the number of Ontario wineries decreased from 67 to 8. Forty-six years would pass before any new licenses were granted.

After World War II everything changed, including public tastes. The demand for sherries and ports dropped and a preference for table wines emerged. Technology and viticultural practices improved and hardier varieties of grapes were found. Diseases and insects had previously devastated vineyards, so growers began to experiment with the more tender viniferas to control these hazards.

By the 1970s, pioneers like Paul Bosc of Chateau des Charmes winery were successfully growing viniferas in Canada. Today, in Ontario, by law, all table wine must be produced exclusively with French hybrids and viniferas. No longer may a commercial table wine from Ontario, sold through the LCBO, contain the old foxy native labrusca grapes.

In 1988 Vintner's Quality Alliance (VQA) — a voluntary alliance of representatives from Ontario's wineries, grape-growers, the LCBO, the academic community, the hospitality industry, and research institutions — set in place rules and regulations governing the quality of Ontario wines.

This appellation controllee system allows Ontario, and now British Columbia, to certify that the wines bearing the VQA medallion and label meet stringent standards of production and taste.

Come with us and discover what consumers and international judges alike are discovering: Canadian table wines are wines of complexity, elegance and finesse.

From Vine to Wine

Wine is mighty to inspire new hopes and wash away
the bitters of care.
Horace, *Carmina, IV,* 13 B.C.

L ike other cool grape-growing regions, such as Oregon and New Zealand, Ontario is surprising the world with its premium wines. An examination of our climate and geography shows why the new breed of winemakers has been able to revolutionize the industry.

14

CLIMATE

Ontario's three wine regions — the Niagara Peninsula, Lake Erie's North Shore, and Pelee Island — are situated in the southern part of the province and subject to the year-round moderating effects of Lake Erie and Lake Ontario.

MICROCLIMATE OF THE NIAGARA PENINSULA

At 43° North latitude the Niagara Peninsula is more southerly than all of the wine areas of France. It is bordered on the north by Lake Ontario and is protected on the south by the Niagara Escarpment. Throughout the year the escarpment is a passive barrier against continental trade winds, while Lake Ontario is an active moderating influence on temperature. It

raises winter temperatures and lowers spring temperatures so that the development of fruit buds is held back until the danger of late-spring frosts has passed. It cools the summer air so that grapes do not ripen too quickly, and then it keeps the fall air comparatively warm so that first frost is delayed and the growing season is extended.

MICROCLIMATE OF THE LAKE ERIE NORTH SHORE REGION

This region is approximately the same latitude as Northern California and the Chianti region of Italy. It runs west from Amherstburg, on the Detroit River, to Leamington. It has no escarpment, and while it enjoys the moderating effects of Lake Erie during the summer and fall, it gets no help during the winter because the lake is so shallow that it often freezes over. Wine-growers here must take special precautions to help their vines survive the winter.

MICROCLIMATE ON PELEE ISLAND

Pelee Island, situated 17 kilometres (11 miles) south of the shoreline, is the most southerly point in Canada. The growing season is 30 days longer than that of the mainland, but because of the cold winter winds off the ice, growers have to take special care of their vines.

As in the rest of Ontario's wine regions, here too it is the cool fall temperatures that give grapes the time they need to develop complex chemical compounds, firm acidity and low pH — perfect elements for quality wines with aging potential and concentrated flavours.

SOIL

The selection of sites for vineyards is influenced by soil (not too rich), drainage (grapes don't like wet feet) and air (circulation is important year-round but especially when the danger of frost exists).

Soil affects the strength of the vine, the time of its maturity, and the quality of the grape. Although classic varietal vines can survive in many soils, they flourish on those considered to be well drained. In these highly permeable and aerated soils, the vines' roots extend deep into the ground, absorbing water and minerals that affect the flavour of the grape and the strength and health of the vine.

Ontario's soils range from sandy loams to gravel and sand, and they are generally considered to be well drained. Where loamy clay soils prevail, drainage methods must be implemented if the land is flat.

PRECIPITATION

Too much rain can cause poor fruit set during flowering, reduce fruit quality and promote fungi. Most fungi (e.g. black rot and downy mildew) are harmful to berries. There is, however, one fungus that wine-growers desire: *Botyris cinera*, also known as noble rot. It is the presence of noble rot that enables winemakers to produce a special type of late-harvest premium wine.

ONTARIO'S GRAPE VARIETIES

The most enjoyable way to expand your knowledge of Ontario wine is to experiment. Sample not only the same varietal wines from different winemakers, but also the same varieties from various climatic zones. For example, the wineries along the "bench" (a small shelf of land halfway up the Niagara Escarpment) produce Rieslings with more pronounced citrus flavours, while the Rieslings from Niagara-on-the-Lake have more peach/apricot characteristics. Lake Erie North Shore Rieslings tend to be

Picking grapes

softer and fuller than Niagara's, thanks to the former's longer growing season and higher heat units.

Compare the same varietals made in completely different styles. Gewürztraminer, for instance, can be spicy but medium dry in the German style or spicy dry in the French Alsatian style.

Sample the same varietal fermented in different ways and/or aged in barrels for varying lengths of time. Chardonnay is probably the most versatile grape variety: it can withstand ice-box or barrel fermentation, long oak or short oak maturation, and even champagnization. Ontario produces a wide range of Chardonnays.

To aid you in your sampling, we have profiled the most popular grape varieties grown and vinified in Ontario.

GRAPE FAMILIES

The three major grape families grown in Ontario are the native North American species, the *Vitis viniferas* of European origin, and the hybrids, crossbred from American and European species.

Among the many North American species, the *Vitis labrusca* predominates, and though they are no longer used in commercial table wines, they are delicious in jellies, jams and juices.

RED VINIFERA VARIETIES

Cabernet Sauvignon (*cab-er-nay so veen yonh*) The premium red grape from Bordeaux ripens late in the season and is more difficult to grow in Ontario; however, many wine-growers are finding success with this variety, known for fullness of character, depth and flavour, combined with high acidity.

Cabernet Franc (*cab-er-nay fronk*) The juice of this honest, unassuming grape of the Cabernet family is used as a blending wine because of its typical Cabernet character (acidity and low tannins). Although lacking the complexity and elegance of Cabernet Sauvignon, it is still vigorous, spicy and herbaceous. Franc is in the experimental-commercial stage in Ontario, but you will see more varietal wines made from this grape in the future.

Merlot (*mair-lo*) In Ontario, Merlot is at its best when produced as a medium-weight but full-bodied wine. It is often used to improve the colour and flavour balance in other red wines. It gives softness and depth to Cabernet-based wines. It is also used in the production of claret.

Pinot Noir (*pee-no nwahr*) The grape of Burgundy, Pinot Noir can only be described as fickle. It is difficult to grow and to vinify, but its black berries produce a fine wine with softness and depth. This wine is always fermented with the skins on to give it added colour and depth. Vinified incorrectly, it can smell like a wet sock; produced properly, it can have hints of plum, violet and strawberry.

Gamay Noir (*ga-may nwahr*) This thin-skinned grape must be vinified with care. It produces a fruity, light-bodied wine, one that can be consumed when young. In Ontario, Gamay Noir is usually produced in the Beaujolais style.

WHITE WINE VINIFERA VARIETIES

Auxerrois (*oh-zair-wah*) This is a very old grape from Burgundy, similar to Chardonnay, grown in Alsace and southern German districts. It makes a crisp wine, light and versatile. Some Ontario winemakers use oak, others go for a more citric character.

Chardonnay (*shar-danay*) Without a doubt the world's most popular variety, Chardonnay can be vinified in a variety of ways and aged for different lengths of time in various types of barrels. Depending on production methods used, Chardonnay has been characterized as rich, complex, nutty, buttery, toasty, herbal and oaky. Aromas show hints of honey, pear, melon and even pineapple.

Riesling (*rees-ling*) Ontario produces some of the best dry Rieslings available today. Rieslings come from the Mosel and Rhine regions of Germany and Alsace. They have a noble aroma with depth of flavour, while retaining their acidity. They show a lot of zest and fruit. Riesling undergoes cool fermentation in stainless steel, usually retaining its identity even when produced in various styles. Floral, herbal and spicy are words often used to describe its personality.

Vidal grapes frozen solid on the vine, prior to picking for icewine

Gewürztraminer (*guh-voortz-trah-mee-ner*) Don't be intimidated by its name. Gewürztraminer is one of the most recognized varieties in the world, variously described as possessing a tropical fruit, spicy or perfumy nose with a refreshingly crisp taste. Its spiciness can be improved if skin contact is employed before fermentation.

HYBRIDS

Hybrids are genetic crosses between different grape varieties. Although it is hard to pinpoint when hybridizing began in Ontario, the most significant benchmark in this province's winemaking took place around 1946. Wine and grape scientist Adhemar de Chaunac from Brights Wines imported 88 red hybrid vines called Marechal Foch from Burgundy, planting them with 200 imported vinifera vines. The venture was successful, and by 1958 Brights Wines had produced their first Burgundy-style wine from these French hybrid grapes.

Two special hybrids are used in wine production: the American hybrid and the vinifera hybrid. American hybrids are crossbred native varieties. Today, only a few varieties (e.g. Veeport and Vincent) are made into fortified "pop" wines. Vinifera hybrids, a cross between the labrusca and the vinifera families, are used in many of our premium table wines.

RED VINIFERA HYBRIDS

de Chaunac (*duh show-nack*) Usually fermented in stainless steel, de Chaunac has been described as fruity and light-bodied with good complexity when barrel-aged. It is spicy, balanced and has great colour, yet in some ways it is a typical hybrid: the approach is great but the finish is lacking in body. Its life span is questionable.

Riesling (left) and Pinot Noir (right) grapes on the vine

Baco Noir (*bah-co nwahr*) At its best when fermented with the skins at a slightly higher temperature and then barrel-aged, Baco Noir produces medium-bodied wine with good colour and a fruity aroma. Baco usually ages beautifully.

Chelois (*shell-wah*) Chelois is fermented in stainless steel and aged briefly in barrels. It produces light-bodied wine with fruity and spicy characteristics.

Marechal Foch (*mar-shall fosh*) Originating in Alsace, Foch is great when produced in the Beaujolais style (using carbonic maceration). It has low acidity, good colour and a soft, pleasant finish. Raspberry and strawberry aromas make it an excellent blending wine.

Villard Noir (*vee-yard nwahr*) Villard is often characterized as dark, medium-bodied and well-balanced. However, it sometimes suffers from being under-ripe. Although this hybrid has been primarily a blending wine in the past, you will see more varietally labelled wines in the future.

WHITE HYBRIDS

Seyval Blanc (*save-al blanh*) This variety produces a well-balanced, medium-bodied white with aromas and flavours reminiscent of citrus, melon and green apple.

Aurore (*aw-roar*) Aurore was developed in France by grape-breeder Albert Seibel. Cold-fermented in stainless steel, Aurore produces a simple wine with fresh, fruity aromas, medium body and a crisp finish.

Vidal (*vee-dal*) Developed by J. L. Vidal in Bordeaux, Vidal is well suited to Ontario's cool climate. Soft, well-balanced and fruity are terms often used to describe this wine. It produces excellent late-harvest wines and Icewines.

Verdelet (*vehr-duh-ley*) A dry, refreshing white.

Winegrower Albrecht Seegar prunes his grapevines

THE WINE-GROWER'S TASK

Let's toast the viticulturalists and wine-growers, for they are the ones who must mediate with Mother Nature. Through various vine-training systems and cultivating techniques, they charm the sun and baffle the frost. A heart-shaped trellising system called the Pendelbogen method is used for vinifera grape varieties. The "bow" originated in Germany, where winters are often harsh. Although recent winters in Ontario's wine country have been relatively mild, wine-growers prefer the bow for winter-sensitive grape varieties such as Chardonnay. In the event of winter damage, more buds are left on the vine and the sensitive grafts remain low enough to the ground to be protected.

The V-shaped French Guyot is the more commonly used training system for vinifera vines. The Guyot exposes the fruit to the air, wind and sunshine. These elements help disease-prone vines.

Most hybrids are trained to the Four-Arm Kniffen system. Here the leaves have a hanging or trailing appearance. The Kniffen lacks foliage support, so the leaves hang over the fruit and block out the sun. (Hybrids are less susceptible to disease and can tolerate the shade.) Wine-growers prefer the Kniffen because less time is required in tying and pruning, and grapes can be harvested mechanically.

Even with proper methods of vine training, wine-growers work extremely hard to get the most out of their vines. You can visit Ontario's wine country during any season and spot wine-growers labouring in their vineyards.

Tying vines to the trellis

In early summer they thin (remove flower clusters) to improve the quality of the fruit and the winter hardiness of the vine, and they sucker to remove superfluous shoots at the base of the vine. During late summer they top their vines (remove the excess growth at the top of the trellis) to better expose the fruit to air, wind and sunshine.

THE WINEMAKER'S TASK

There are basically six processes in the transformation of grapes into wine: harvesting, crushing, pressing, fermentation, clarification, and maturation. Vinification is responsible for at least half of the final quality of the wine. Winemakers adamantly agree that premium wine can be made only with premium grapes. Even a great vintage can be spoiled by winemaking errors such as harvesting grapes too early or too late, haphazard fermentation practices, or unclean conditions.

The final quality of the wine depends not only on what winemakers do, but also on what they refrain from doing. Knowing when to act decisively and when to surrender to nature's wisdom is perhaps a winemaker's most daunting challenge. Decisions have to be made at every stage of the process, and they are a balancing act between science and art, knowledge and taste.

HARVESTING

As grapes ripen they produce higher concentrations of sugar (measured in brix) and flavour, while producing less acid. A long, cool growing season provides optimal conditions, but few seasons are perfect, and the winemaker must decide when the grapes are at their peak.

A cold growing season produces ripened grapes with low sugar and high acidity. No amount of time on the vine will ripen them further. A warm,

Grapes go into the crusher at Henry of Pelham winery

humid season can produce high sugars with low acidity but will also make the grapes more susceptible to disease.

It is best to pick grapes on cool days or in the early morning. To prevent oxidation (not as much a problem with reds as with whites) and unwanted yeasts and bacteria, the time between picking and crushing is kept as short as possible.

Picking by hand is preferable because of the control it allows: damaged, mouldy or decayed berries can be culled. But handpicking is slow and expensive compared to mechanical harvesters, which can pick up to six tons of grapes per hour using flexible rods that "slap" the vines and shake the berries free into catching frames.

In a good year, grapes left longer on the vine will develop more sugar and more concentrated flavours. These late-harvested grapes can produce wines of very fine quality. If conditions are very cool and dry, late-harvested grapes can become infected with a surface fungus (Botrytis, or noble rot) which will extract moisture from the grapes and leave highly concentrated flavours.

The sweetest and most elegant of all late-harvested wines is the Icewine. Ontario winemakers are quickly gaining international prestige with their award-winning Icewines, made from frost-affected grapes picked as late as January or February.

In Ontario, Icewine is made from white grapes with thicker skins than most, such as Gewürztraminer, Vidal or Riesling. The juice for this exceptional wine must be pressed quickly before the ice crystals thaw.

CRUSHING

As soon as the grapes come in from the vineyard, they are dumped into the crusher/destemmer, where the skins are gently broken and the stalks are removed. The stalks contain bitter-tasting phenols which can affect the quality of the wine. Some wines, however, such as Pinot Noir, may benefit from the retention of stalks.

In some cases, the winemaker may choose not to crush the berries until they have fermented first, using a process called carbonic maceration. Whole bunches of grapes are placed into a vat of carbon dioxide, where a different kind of fermentation starts inside the grape. This process causes richer colour and soft flavours in the wine.

PRESSING

The degree of pressing affects the quality of the wine: the gentler the better. The finest wines are produced from the free-run juice (as a natural result of the grapes' own weight combined with the initial light pressing).

Most presses are pneumatically or electrically operated. A balloon or inflated rubber bag gently forces the grapes against a cylinder. The grapes are then compressed to separate the juice from the skins, seeds and pulp.

FERMENTATION

The basis for all wine-making is a simple biochemical reaction. A sugar solution is allowed to ferment, thereby producing alcohol and carbon-dioxide gas while releasing heat.

Fermentation is caused by yeast. There are numerous kinds of yeast, both natural and cultured. In many old European wineries, natural airborne yeasts that are beneficial to wine have developed over hundreds of years. But in our comparatively young Canadian wineries, airborne yeasts are not beneficial to wine and can cause spoilage, so winemakers introduce cultured yeasts into the juice to start the fermentation.

The juice from pressed grapes is placed into insulated vats made of a material such as stainless steel or oak, but never in a permeable material such as copper or iron. The fermentation temperature must then be controlled. The higher the temperature of the fermenting juice (called "must"), the quicker the reaction.

Under warm conditions (20-25°C/68-77°F) the fermentation usually takes about two weeks; under cool conditions (below 20°C/68°F) it takes three weeks. Excessive amounts of bitter tannins and phenols may be released and spoil the flavour if temperatures exceed 25°C/77°F.

Only the juice for white wines is placed in the fermenting vats. Sweet wine is produced by stopping the fermentation before all of the sugar is converted; full fermentation produces sparkling wine; and conversion of all sugar produces dry wine.

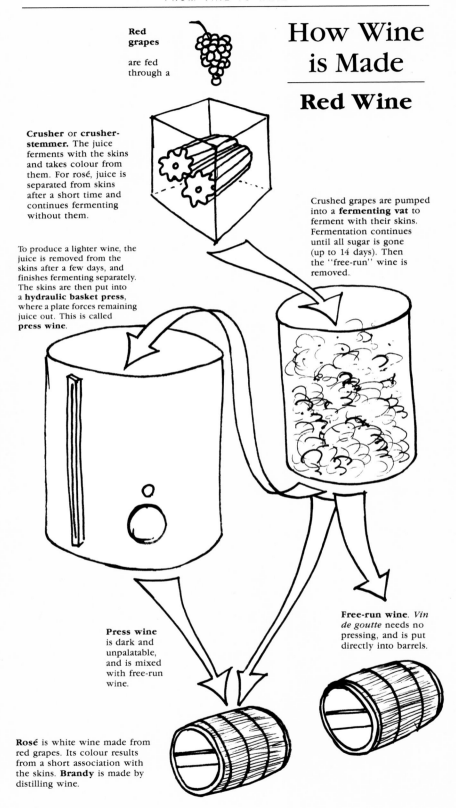

Red grapes

are fed through a

How Wine is Made

Red Wine

Crusher or **crusher-stemmer.** The juice ferments with the skins and takes colour from them. For rosé, juice is separated from skins after a short time and continues fermenting without them.

Crushed grapes are pumped into a **fermenting vat** to ferment with their skins. Fermentation continues until all sugar is gone (up to 14 days). Then the "free-run" wine is removed.

To produce a lighter wine, the juice is removed from the skins after a few days, and finishes fermenting separately. The skins are then put into a **hydraulic basket press**, where a plate forces remaining juice out. This is called **press wine**.

Free-run wine. *Vin de goutte* needs no pressing, and is put directly into barrels.

Press wine is dark and unpalatable, and is mixed with free-run wine.

Rosé is white wine made from red grapes. Its colour results from a short association with the skins. **Brandy** is made by distilling wine.

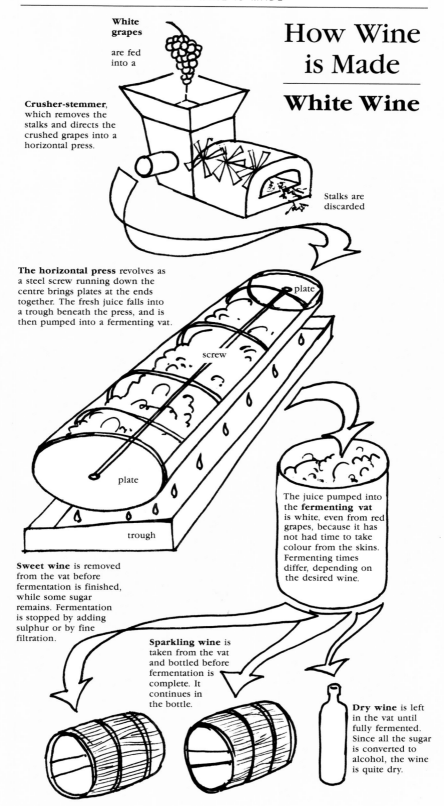

How Wine is Made

White Wine

White grapes are fed into a

Crusher-stemmer, which removes the stalks and directs the crushed grapes into a horizontal press.

Stalks are discarded

The horizontal press revolves as a steel screw running down the centre brings plates at the ends together. The fresh juice falls into a trough beneath the press, and is then pumped into a fermenting vat.

plate

screw

plate

trough

The juice pumped into the **fermenting vat** is white, even from red grapes, because it has not had time to take colour from the skins. Fermenting times differ, depending on the desired wine.

Sweet wine is removed from the vat before fermentation is finished, while some sugar remains. Fermentation is stopped by adding sulphur or by fine filtration.

Sparkling wine is taken from the vat and bottled before fermentation is complete. It continues in the bottle.

Dry wine is left in the vat until fully fermented. Since all the sugar is converted to alcohol, the wine is quite dry.

27

Putting grapes into the destemmer

Red wines are pumped into a primary fermentation tank after destemming, but with the skins on in order to extract some colour. The skins also give red wine tannin and other characteristics.

After primary fermentation, the red wine berries are pumped into a press for hot pressing. The resulting juice is pumped into a vat for secondary fermentation, then pumped into barrels for aging.

CLARIFICATION

After fermentation stops, minute particles remain in suspension until they are removed by racking, fining and filtering.

Racking is the syphoning of the wine from the lees (sediment). Fining is the addition of a coagulant such as egg white, bentonite, etc., which causes suspended particles to sink. Filtering removes suspended and settled particles by means of cellulose meshes. A centrifuge can also be used to achieve these results, probably with less chance of removing any flavour or aroma.

MATURATION (Storing and Aging)

White wines can be stored in stainless steel, mature oak or glass bottles. Six months is the optimum time for most whites, but complex whites like Riesling and Chardonnay can improve with age and often benefit from oak. Sweeter late-harvest wines and Icewines improve delightfully with several years' storage. Red wine is aged one or two years before bottling.

The barrel room at Brights Wines

BOTTLING AND CORKING

Bottling is stressful for the wine, with many potential problems. For instance, too much oxygen or unknown micro-organisms can enter the wine. Advanced bottling systems and equipment help to prevent these problems, but every step must be monitored with care.

Cork's fine internal structure, low density, compressibility, impermeability and endurance make it a perfect stopper for wine. Screw caps, on the other hand, demand high precision in the moulding of the bottle neck and seem better suited to wines that will have a short life.

STORING AND SERVING WINES AT HOME

Store all bottled wines on their sides in cool, dry conditions. Moist corks remain firm and prevent air from entering the bottles and oxidizing the wines. Wine ages more quickly in warm conditions.

Decant wine by pouring it from the bottle into a carafe. The wine will age in a matter of hours as the oxygen comes into contact and brings out its full flavour and aroma. This is especially good for young wine, but a better gauge is that the more full-bodied the wine, the longer it takes to breathe.

The aromatics of red wine are released at cool temperatures, but cold will inhibit their volatile vapours. Cabernet Franc, Merlot, Cabernet Sauvignon, Marechal Foch and Baco Noir all benefit from cool room temperature. Lighter reds like Gamay Noir and Pinot Noir can be served cooler still but not cold.

White wines should be served cold, either from the refrigerator or from an ice bucket. The sweeter the wine, the colder it should be served.

Wine is more than just a beverage; every glass is a story of dedication, risk, patience and passion. Salut!

Visiting Wineries

Wine is the most healthful and most hygenic of beverages.
Louis Pasteur (1822-95)

Discovering Ontario's Wine Country is organized according to geographic areas to make planning your visit easier. We also offer the following suggestions.

CHOICE

We recommend that you balance your tour by visiting one of the larger wineries (Brights, Andrés, Hillebrand, Inniskillin) and some of the smaller ones. Larger wineries have regularly scheduled tours, but smaller operators need a call ahead of time if you want to be sure to meet the winemaker. Spend one-half to two hours per winery; wine-tasting can be exhausting if you crowd too many into a day. Some wineries, such as Stoney Ridge and Vineland Estates, serve light lunches.

Wine expert Andrew Sharp

The wine boutique at Reif Estate Winery

TASTING WINE

Start by examining what you see, then what you smell, what you feel, and last of all, what you taste. Nothing is more critical to wine-tasting than a "sense-itive" taster. By using key questions to guide your evaluation, you will understand why you liked or disliked a particular wine. Wines differ in colour, texture, strength, body and aroma, as well as taste.

The chart on page 32 is the evaluation system used by international tasters at the renowned InterVin competition. It was developed by Andrew Sharp. Consult his book, *Intervin Guide to Award-Winning Wines* (1990), for more on his "winetaster's secrets." Another reliable source is Michael Broadbent's handy *Pocket Guide to Wine Tasting* (1988) or the *Academie du Vin Wine Course* by Steven Spurrier and Michael Dovaz (1990). These sources will teach you how to match words to what you are sensing.

ETIQUETTE

When on tour, eliminate extraneous odours and flavours that might interfere with your ability to discern aroma and taste. Avoid gum, candy, perfume and cigarettes. Above all, be attentive and ask lots of questions. If you see Uncle Harry chug-a-lugging his Chardonnay, take him aside. Also remember that proprietors don't expect you to like everything they serve, so feel free to leave some samples after just a taste.

Spitting out wine is not an indication of disregard. On the contrary, it is a recognized ritual of wine-tasting and most wineries provide a bucket or sink for that purpose. It is also wise to keep consumption low when on

InterVin

NUMERICAL EVALUATION SYSTEM

	GREAT	FINE	ORDINARY	POOR	UNACCEPTABLE	
VISUAL SURFACE	4	3	2	1	0	bright — reflective — dull — clean — iridescent — faulty
CLARITY/LIMPIDITY	4	3	2	1	0	brilliant — bright — clear — dull — hazy — cloudy no deposit — visible deposits effervescent wines: fine, steady effervescence — rapid, large, coarse bubbles — light, slow effervescence
DEPTH/LUMINANCE	4	3	2	1	0	watery — pale — light — medium — dark — opaque
TINT/HUE	4	3	2	1	0	(RED) purple — purple red — ruby red — garnet red — red brown — mahogany — amber brown (ROSÉ) solid rosé — pale red — pink tints — purple tints — blue tints — orange tints — onion skin (WHITE) greenish tints — light yellow — yellow — yellow gold — gold — gold brown — amber
OLFACTORY (NOSE) INTENSITY/PURITY	4	3	2	1	0	neutral — light — ordinary — intense — very intense — overpowering clean — pleasant — unpleasant — faulty
AROMA	4	3	2	1	0	neutral — light — fruity — varietally distinctive — classically varietal
BOUQUET	8	6	4	2	0	simple, vinous — moderate development — complex — intense — powerful — excessive (e.g. too woody, yeasty, etc.)
HARMONY/BALANCE	8	6	4	2	0	very unbalanced — slightly unbalanced — good harmony — perfectly harmonious
TACTILE (TOUCH) BODY	8	6	4	2	0	thin, watery — light — medium structure — full-bodied — heavy — excessively heavy effervescent wines: petillant — crackling — sparkling coarse — ordinary — mousse-like
ASTRINGENCY	4	3	2	1	0	excessively astringent — astringent — hard — dry — soft — mature
TASTE (GUSTATORY) INTENSITY/PURITY	4	3	2	1	0	neutral — light — ordinary — intense — powerful clean — pleasant — unpleasant — faulty
SWEETNESS	4	3	2	1	0	austere — dry — medium dry — medium sweet — very sweet
ACIDITY	8	6	4	2	0	dull — flabby — balanced — fresh — tart — excessively acidic — green — acetic fault
BITTERNESS	4	3	2	1	0	none — faint — moderate — strongly evident — offensive
HARMONY/BALANCE	8	6	4	2	0	very unbalanced — slightly unbalanced — good harmony — perfectly harmonious
FLAVOR (NOSE + TASTE) AFTERTASTE	4	3	2	1	0	none — elusive — moderate — distinctive clean — faulty
PERSISTENCE	8	6	4	2	0	short — medium — long — very long — too persistent
OVERALL QUALITY	8	6	4	2	0	unacceptable — poor — acceptable — ordinary — good — very good, fine — excellent, great, outstanding
				0		**TOTAL SCORE**

COLUMN TOTAL

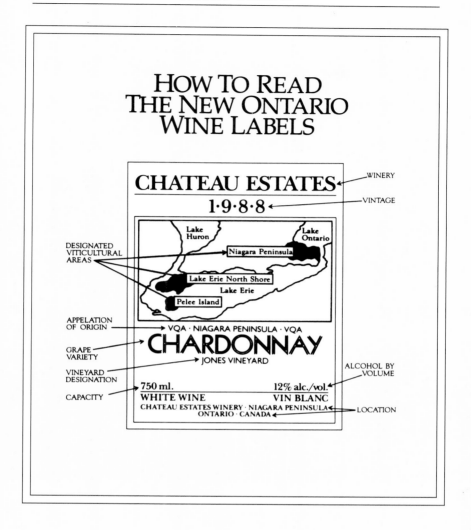

the road, not just for drivers, but also for passengers, who may doze off and miss part of the trip.

Unruly children, crying infants, know-it-all wine buffs, and gabby talkers who ignore the tour guide can ruin an otherwise pleasant and informative visit, so keep your crew under control. And remember that winemakers have feelings; be sensitive when you pass judgement on their art.

BUYING WINE

Remember that wine will "cook" in a closed car on a hot or sunny day. Also, loose bottles may break, so bring along newspaper for packing. You may pay for your wine at the winery shop with a credit card, even on Sunday.

Ontario is best known for its crisp whites, especially the Rieslings and Chardonnays, not to mention its international award-winning Icewines. But the province also produces some fine sparkling wines, and the Pinot Noir, Cabernet Franc and Merlot show tremendous elegance among the reds.

Touring the Niagara Peninsula

A Book of Verses underneath the Bough,
A Jug of Wine, a Loaf of Bread — and Thou
Beside me singing in the Wilderness —
Oh, wilderness were Paradise enow!...

And much as Wine has play'd the Infidel,
And robb'd me of my Robe of Honor — Well
I wonder often what the Vintners buy
One half so precious as the stuff they sell.

from *The Rubiayat of Omar Khayyam*

Wineries West of the Welland Canal

THE NIAGARA WINE ROUTE runs from Stoney Creek to Niagara Falls. The six wineries between St. Catharines and Hamilton are easily accessible from the QEW. A more scenic and leisurely approach is from Regional Highway 81, or the old No. 8 highway as locals call it. This is the old Grimsby–Queenston Road which linked the main villages along the lakeshore and served as the major route between Niagara and Toronto from the early 1800s until the QEW was built. Today it is a road of fruit stands, specialty shops, orchards, elegant old homes, historic churches, farms, restaurants and watering holes. It is also home to some of the most interesting wine cellars (and sellers) in Canada. A perfect place to start a tour.

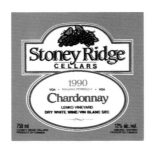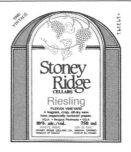

Stoney Ridge Cellars

A t the western edge of Niagara, at Winona, is Stoney Ridge Cellars, the farm winery by the escarpment. Winemaker Jim Warren has had the attention of wine-lovers and critics alike since the winery opened in 1986.

This little boutique operation (30,000 gallons / 114,000 litres a year) has been bringing home the gold at international competitions for its rich, full-bodied Chardonnay and its fruity, well-balanced Carbernet Franc and Merlot.

"Five years ago," says Warren, "they would have said, 'You'll never get a good red out of Ontario,' or 'You'll never get a Chardonnay as good as the French,' but we're doing it and proving it."

The grapes that go into Stoney Ridge wines come from either the winery vineyards or from growers on the Beamsville Bench nearby. Warren's partner is grape-grower Murray Puddicombe, whose vineyard farm has been in the family since Puddicombe's United Empire Loyalist ancestors were first granted these Crown lands. On pleasant days, visitors can take a wagon ride to his escarpment vineyards.

The fruit market and wine boutique

Winemaker Jim Warren and grower Murray Puddicombe

Puddicombe and Warren have transformed an old on-site farm building into a romantic touring facility. A fruit market on one side of the building sells fruits as well as pâté, cheeses and fresh breads. A second-floor balcony surrounds the winery, where visitors can have lunch and enjoy any one of Stoney Ridge's 25 different wines.

Stoney Ridge uses both French hybrid and vinifera grapes in their wines. Some, such as Morio Muscat, French Colombard and Jasmine, are seldom found in Ontario. They are able to boast more wines listed with the VQA than any other winery in Ontario. Given their size, that's quite a testimony to their quality. Most of their wine is sold at the cellar door since production is limited.

Stoney Ridge Cellars
1468 Hwy 8
Winona, Ont. L0R 2L0
(416) 643-4508
or (416) 383-3982 eve.
Fax (416) 643-0933

Wine Boutique: Sun-Mon 10:00-5:00

Tours:
By appointment

Directions:
QEW exit #78, go south on Fifty Rd., then east on Hwy 8.

Andrés Wines Ltd.

A ndrés, Canada's second-largest winery, produces a clean and easy-drinking line of generic wines broadly known throughout Ontario. With products such as Hochtaler and Domaine D'or, Andrés captures about 35 percent of the domestic market.

Having no corporate vineyards of its own, Andrés produces no estate wines, but 85 percent of grapes purchased are grown in Ontario, and winemaker Barry Poag makes a number of excellent VQA-listed varietals. Their distinction, however, is versatility and quality control on a larger scale. "Our focus has been in producing, from grapes grown in the Niagara Peninsula, well-made, clean wines of excellent quality and value." Poag hopes visitors will feel unintimidated by the winery's size.

Andrés was founded in 1961 by its present owner, Andrew Peller, who gave it his first name but with a French twist. It continues to be a family-owned company, with son and grandson now in charge. The Pellers'

Winemaker Barry Poag

The bottling line at Andrés Wines

philosophy has always been to follow the tastes of the consumer rather than to dictate it, but they have been careful not to compromise their own influence on production standards and quality.

When Canadians wanted to switch from beer and heavy fortifieds, Andrés gave them Baby Duck, a light sparkling wine. When Canadians wanted an easy, clean white table wine, Andrés gave them Hochtaler and Domaine D'or. Andrés' most recent addition to the market is their wine-based liqueurs, Panama Jack, Irish Cream and Pina Colada.

The highlight of this tour is Andrés' bottling operation, which can be viewed clearly from an elevated platform. They also have a variety of touring packages, from regularly scheduled public tours to deluxe packages that offer dinner parties and executive meeting and hospitality rooms.

Andrés Wines Ltd. 697 South Service Rd. P.O. Box 550 Winona, Ont. L0R 2L0 (416) 643-4131 or 1-800-263-2170 Fax (416) 643-4944	**Tours:** Mon-Fri 11:30 & 2:30 Sat & Sun 1:00 & 3:00 (Group tours pre-arranged)
Wine Boutique: Mon-Fri 10:00-5:00 Sat & Sun 12:00-6:00	**Directions:** QEW exit #78, go south on Fifty Rd., then east on South Service Rd.

Montravin

The origins of this winery date back to 1973, when third-generation wine-maker Karl Podamer was first granted a license to produce champagne-style sparkling wine. Podamer was granted his commercial license in 1975. In 1983 Podamer Winery was renamed Montravin, but Podamer's name remains on the label of its premium champagnes to honour his legacy.

Austrian-born oenologist Ernst Fischer, with experience on three continents, took over as winemaker for Montravin, adding new styles but still using the time-honoured *methode Champénoise* to make the prize-winning Podamer line.

There are several ways to make sparkling wines. The difference is in the grapes used, the method of fermentation, and the length of time the wine lies on the yeast sediment. In *methode Champénoise*, the wine never leaves the bottle, staying on its lees for two to three years.

Don't be fooled by Montravin's inauspicious front. Inside you'll see a large production facility and be given a fascinating tour through each step of the champagne-making process, from the blending of the cuvée to clarification, from tirage (the addition of sweet syrup, then drawn off into bottles) to secondary fermentation and riddling (the daily turning of bottles on racks to gradually get the yeast sediment to sink to the cork, leaving the wine clear), and on to the disgorging of the sediment (freezing the neck and replacing the loss with a secret recipe of sweet liquor or sweetener).

Fischer's second line of Montravin sparkling wine is made using the Charmat method, which ferments the wine in large holding tanks before bottling.

Podamer bottles

Montravin
4701 Ontario St.
Beamsville, Ont. L0R 1B4
(416) 563-5313
Fax (416) 563-8804

Wine Boutique:
Mon-Fri 9:00-12:00, 1:00-5:00

Tours:
By appointment

Directions:
QEW exit #64, go south on
Ontario St.

Vineland Estates

The most romantic of Ontario's wineries, Vineland Estates is located on the highest point of its St. Urban vineyards, behind a century oak on the rolling landscape of the Beamsville Bench. This could be Napa or Burgundy, but it's Niagara at its best. From Vineland's wine deck you can see compelling stretches of Lake Ontario and feel the continuous breezes blowing off the water.

Winery president Herman Weis, a Mosel winemaker and nurseryman (Weis Nurseries are the largest private grapevine nurseries in Germany), first planted his own Riesling vines in 1977 in this St. Urban vineyard. The first wines were bottled for commercial sales by 1983.

Allan Schmidt, winemaker and winery manager, joined the winery in 1987 and continues to produce estate Rieslings that show a unique regional character resulting from the microclimate of the Bench. Similar to those from the Mosel-Saar-Ruwer region in Germany, his Rieslings have a herbaceous fruitiness with steely acidity and rich, full-bodied flavour.

Vineland Estates sales director Anne Weis

42

Winemaker Allan Schmidt at a summer barbecue at the winery

Enjoying the wine bar

Besides producing some of the finest Rieslings in Canada, Vineland Estates was the first winery to incorporate a wine bistro, in the enclosed front porch of their 1845 farmhouse. Enjoy a serene afternoon's lunch in the country.

They have also converted an old cottage nearby into a self-contained bed and breakfast operation. If you call ahead, they will even prepare a vineyard picnic for you.

Vineland Estates	**Tours:**
RR #3, Moyer Rd.	May-Oct 11:00 & 1:00 & 3:00
Vineland, Ont. L0R 2C0	Nov-Sept (By appointment)
(416) 562-7088	
Fax (416) 562-3071	**Directions:**
	QEW exit #57, go south on
Wine Boutique: Sun-Mon 10:00-5:00	Victoria Ave., then west on Moyer Rd.

Cave Spring Cellars

O n the main street of Jordan, a tiny jewel of a village on the edge of one of the escarpment's most majestic wooded valleys, is yet another jewel, Cave Spring Cellars.

Cave Spring is one of the most critically praised of the new Canadian wineries. Since opening in 1987, it has assumed a significant leadership role in demonstrating that the quality of Canadian wines can be measured successfully not only against international standards of excellence, but also against a Canadian identity all their own.

By vinifying only 100-percent vinifera grapes grown on the Beamsville Bench, Cave Spring illustrates the connection between a wine's origins and its quality. Says President Leonard Pennachetti, "Our wines capture what the French call a *goût de terroir*, or 'taste of the soil' from which they come, and no amount of artifice — viticultural, oenological or otherwise — could ever replicate the particular flavour profile they achieve."

The quiet town of Jordan

44

President Len Pennachetti and winemaker Angelo Pavan

That profile has been described as racy, herbaceous and/or grapefruit-like, with refreshing acidity and a peach-like bouquet. Through very gentle pressing, Cave Spring extracts only the most delicate flavours from their grapes. They then shepherd the wines through a long, cool fermentation to preserve the true varietal characters.

Cave Spring Cellars trusts the Bench's microclimate (no air pockets, minimum frost, low humidity, good drainage, later ripening) and clay loam soils to produce delicious fruit unique to their area of Niagara. "This winery exists because of the vineyards," says winemaker Angelo Pavan, a lifelong friend of Pennachetti.

Their Chardonnay Reserve and off-dry Riesling have received special recognition as possessing outstanding elegance, concentration and complexity. All of their wines are produced according to VQA standards.

Cave Spring Cellars
3836 Main St.
Jordan, Ont. L0R 1S0
(416) 562-3581
Call for Fax number

Wine Boutique:
Mon-Sat 10:00-5:00
Sun 12:00-5:00

Tours:
July-Oct Sat & Sun 1:00
Nov-June (By appointment)

Directions: QEW exit #24, go south on Victoria Ave., then east on Hwy 81, at top of valley but before Jordan Hotel turn north on Main Street.

Henry of Pelham

A t the junction of Effingham and Pelham roads in St. Catharines stands the old tollgate and inn of Henry Smith. In 1842 he built this inn on the Crown lands awarded to his father, Nicholas Smith, a bugler with the famous Butler's Rangers. Generations of Smiths square-danced in its ballroom upstairs. It has since been restored by Henry's descendants Paul and Bobbi Speck and their three sons, and today the inn houses their wine store and cooperage. Also planned are a restaurant and a wine school.

Henry of Pelham's vineyards of French hybrids and viniferas are situated at the north end of the Short Hills on the Niagara Bench, crisscrossing some of the most picturesque rolling hills in Niagara.

Ron Giesbrecht, the resident winemaker, has great affinity for the area. Born in Vineland, only minutes away, Giesbrecht has spent a lifetime on the Bench and knows its promise by heart.

"We're able to get better results with our grapes," explains Giesbrecht, a microbiologist and oenologist who studied at the University of Guelph,

Winemaker Ron Giesbrecht

46

A reminder of earlier times

"because we're able to leave them on the vine longer. That enables them to develop the flavours and aromatic chemicals they need to give wines true distinction."

Giesbrecht combines the passion of a native son with the expertise of a scientist. He believes in subjective creativity. "How cool is cool when fermentation begins? When does a winemaker rack? When should he bottle?" asks Giesbrecht. "All of these operations involve a great deal of science, which allows each operation to be repeated when necessary, but the art of winemaking is the ultimate challenge and the palate is the ultimate tool."

Henry of Pelham's barrel-fermented Chardonnays show tropical fruit flavours with subtle hints of oak and good acidity, and their Baco Noir is a fresh yet robust red reminiscent of a rich Chianti.

The winery's scenic escarpment location, combined with its state-of-the-art equipment and focus on education, makes Henry of Pelham a most interesting tour.

Henry of Pelham
1469 Pelham Rd.
St. Catharines, Ont. L2R 6P7
(416) 684-8423
Fax (416) 684-8444

Wine Boutique:
Sun-Mon 10:00-6:00

Tours:
Mon-Fri 11:30 & 1:30 & 3:30
Sat & Sun 12:00 & 2:00 & 4:00

Directions: QEW exit #51, go south on 7th St., then east on Hwy 81, then south on 5th St. to junction of Effingham & Pelham Rd.

*A laker going through
the Welland Canal (above)*

Wineries East of the Welland Canal

THE WINERIES EAST of the Welland Canal are located predominantly in Niagara-on-the-Lake and Niagara Falls. Besides the magnificent Falls, there are places and events that visitors should not miss, such as the Shaw Festival Theatre's summer repertory series and the 19th-century architectural heritage of Niagara-on-the-Lake, with its shops, restaurants and gentle charm. The surrounding countryside consists of the richest farmland in Canada. This is Canada's cornucopia — graceful orchards of peaches, cherries, plums, apples and grapes line back roads that most visitors never travel. Let the wine route take you there.

49

Chateau des Charmes

Paul Michel Bosc Sr., French-trained winemaker and co-owner of Chateau des Charmes, is not only well-known for his award-winning Estate Pinot Noir and Champagne Sec, but is renowned for having changed the direction of grape-growing in Canada.

During the late seventies, viticultural researchers believed Niagara's climatic conditions were too harsh for growing European *Vitis vinifera* grape varieties. They advised commercial grape farmers to plant only a few of these vines until further research could be conducted. Bosc believed otherwise. He had worked with viniferas and knew they could grow on the peninsula, where temperatures were similar to those of Champagne and Burgundy. Chateau des Charmes' other co-owner, lawyer and part-time farmer Roger Gordon, trusted Bosc's judgement and planted their 24-hectare (60-acre) vineyard exclusively to viniferas.

The venture was successful and commercial wine-growers across Canada began to follow suit. Bosc attributes his success to the five generations of viticultural and vinicultural knowledge he acquired through his family and his years of practical experience.

His great-great-grandparents were French winemakers who moved to Algeria in 1840 to start up the first vineyard in Marengo. As a child, Bosc helped his father maintain the vineyards. He attended the University of Dijon in Burgundy, graduated as an oenologist, and managed a co-operative winery in Algeria. After immigrating to Canada, he spent 15 years as Chateau-Gai's chief winemaker and director of research.

In 1978 Bosc opened Chateau des Charmes. This winery was the first on the peninsula to perfect an untraditional vinification process called carbonic maceration. In this method, uncrushed grapes and a special *primeur* yeast imported from France are put into a sealed fermentation tank. "The weight of the grapes causes the berries at the bottom of the tank to crack," explains Bosc. "The juice comes into contact with the yeast, the fermentation process begins, and carbon dioxide is produced. Carbonic maceration reduces the amount of malic acid in the juice, which makes the resulting wine smoother."

Winemaker and owner Paul Bosc

Gamay Nouveau is an example of a wine fermented using carbonic maceration. This fresh and fruity wine has low acidity and should be consumed within a year.

Chateau des Charmes' future is most promising. They plan to double production at a winery to be located on a 38-hectare (93-acre) vineyard on the St. David's Bench. The sprawling chateau will include a state-of-the-art production facility and hospitality centre containing a theatre, wine museum, retail store and wine bar.

Chateau des Charmes
P.O. Box 280
St. Davids, Ont. L0S 1P0
(416) 262-4219 or 1-800-263-2541
Fax (416) 262-5548

Wine Boutique:
Mon-Sun 9:00-5:00

Tours:
May-Sept 11:00 & 1:30 & 3:00
Oct-April (By appointment)

Directions: QEW exit #32B, go east on Hwy 8A (York Rd.), then north on Creek Rd. Winery on east side near Line 7.

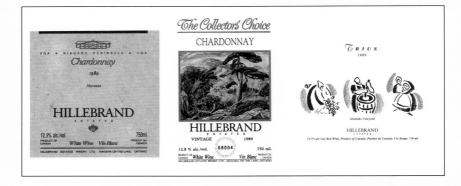

Hillebrand Estates

Through well-managed and well-integrated cellar-working principles, Hillebrand has moved from being a young, relatively unknown winery to becoming one of Canada's top producers of exceptionally clean and complex varietal wines.

Hillebrand's tradition stems from its sister companies Scholl & Hillebrand, Schlumberger, and Blanc Foussy of Europe. Their well-established wine estates provide over a century of winemaking expertise.

Hillebrand calls its winemaking style "multicultural" because, between them, winemakers Laurent Dal'Zovo, Jean-Laurent Groux and Robert Mielzynski have studied in France, Germany and California. They collaborate as winemakers to produce dry, elegant Canadian wines.

Although its own vineyards are devoted to viticultural experimentation, Hillebrand works very closely with 45 growers in the Niagara region, giving regular seminars and instruction on the latest viticultural procedures. Because it obtains grapes from many producers, Hillebrand can select only the best. Its winemakers are able to distinguish between the three growing

Scott Moore harvesting grapes for Icewine

regions of Niagara (the bench, lakeshore and Niagara-on-the-Lake) and can detect in the grape the differences that soil, climate and location create.

Hillebrand places great emphasis on educating its staff as well as the consumer. They have developed extensive educational materials and comprehensive touring facilities.

Besides selling their wines at their own boutique and in provincial LCBO outlets, Hillebrand promotes its wines in 44 retail stores in Ontario.

Its new sister company, Mounier, on the same site but considered a separate operation, produces high-quality champagne using only vinifera grapes in the time-honoured *methode Champénoise.*

Hillebrand Estates	**Tours:**
RR #2, Hwy 55	Daily 11:00 & 1:00 & 3:00 & 4:00
Niagara-on-the-Lake, Ont. L0S 1J0	
(416) 468-3201	**Directions:** QEW exit #38A, go
Fax (416) 468-4789	north on Hwy 55. Winery before
	Virgil.
Wine Boutique: Sun-Mon 10:00-6:00	

Stonechurch Vineyards

R ick Hunse and family have joined the ranks of those diligent grape-growers who have moved from supplying top-quality grapes to other wineries to producing wines of their own.

Hunse joined forces with winemaker David Hulley, the first Canadian to graduate in oenology from the prestigious University of California at Davis. Hunse and Hulley aim to pull out all the stops in their attempt to produce quality wines. "Great wines are made in the vineyard," says Hulley. "Hunse's vineyards are like manicured putting greens — pristine and personally well-tended. For a winemaker, that really means a lot, because it is an indication that the grapes are not just being grown as a commodity; there is something more personal going on."

Balance is the key to Hulley's winemaking philosophy. "I am a facilitator, not a dominator," says Hulley. "I believe it's important to work within nature's own balance, not to oppose it or dominate it by putting my thumbprint on every wine I make. Wine tells you something new with every vintage."

Stonechurch wines have already started to show distinction, particularly their barrel-fermented Chardonnay. Because it has extended lees contact, it has a large, toasty, buttery richness which is unique for the area. Their Pinot Noir also has extraordinarily concentrated flavours.

Their wines are made from 100-percent Ontario grapes and are estate-bottled. Besides noble varieties such as Cabernet Sauvignon and Merlot, they also produce Morio Muscat, a dry wine with nuances of clove and nutmeg, and a citric finish. Hunse is one of only a very few growers in Canada who grow this variety.

The winery is named after an old 19th-century stone church that sits near the corner of the Hunse farm. Legend has it that during prohibition the farm's underground caves served as sanctuary to rumrunning smugglers. Hunse and Hulley's aim for excellence is much more reverent, even if it is less "spirit-ual"!

Winemaker David Hulley with owner and grower Rick Hunse

Stonechurch Vineyards
1270 Irvine Rd.
Niagara-on-the-Lake, Ont. L0S 1J0
(416) 935-3535
Fax (416) 646-8892

Wine Boutique:
April-Dec (Mon-Sat) 10:00-6:00
Jan-Mar (Thurs-Sat) 10:00 - 5:00

Tours:
By appointment
Vineyard Excursion

Directions: QEW exit Niagara St.,
go north, then east on Lakeshore
Rd., then south on Irvine Rd.
Winery 200 m from Lakeshore
& Irvine.

Konzelmann Estate Winery

Konzelmann Estate Winery offers a unique wine tour. President, winemaker and owner Herbert Konzelmann guides you on a personalized tour of his vineyard and winery. He explains viticulture and viniculture in Ontario and answers any questions you may have regarding grapes and wine. At the end of the tour, you may sample his wines.

Konzelmann makes a wide spectrum of wines, ranging from a very dry Chardonnay to a rich dessert wine called Icewine. Made from grapes harvested in winter, the Icewine has won several gold medals at the InterVin International Wine Competition and the Wine and Cheese Show in Toronto. Konzelmann has also won awards for his other wines, including InterVin's bronze medal for his Gewürztraminer. Most of Konzelmann's products are sweetened with the unfermented grape juice. All are estate-bottled.

Konzelmann was educated in winemaking at the Wein Bauschule in Weinsberg, Germany, and went on to run the family winery founded by his great-grandfather Friedrich Konzelmann. It was during a hunting trip to Canada that Herbert Konzelmann fell in love with this country and discovered that there were wine regions to be found here as well. On a

Herbert Konzelmann, owner and winemaker

second visit to Canada, Konzelmann toured the Okanagan Valley with the intention of buying property. Instead, he found what he was looking for on the Niagara Peninsula — a 16-hectare (40-acre) plot fronting Lake Ontario. In 1983 he officially immigrated to Canada and began to plant his vineyard with 30,000 vinifera vines.

Konzelmann was the first wine-grower to introduce Vertico training to Canada. Among its many advantages, this method allows the sun and wind to go through the vines, thus drying off morning dew and rain. So far, Vertico training has worked well for Konzelmann Estate winery.

Konzelmann Estate Winery
RR#3 Lakeshore Rd.
Niagara-on-the-Lake, Ont. L0S 1J0
(416) 935-2866
Fax (416) 935-2864

Wine Boutique:
Jan-Mar (Wed-Sat) 10:00-6:00
April (Mon-Sat) 10:00-6:00
May-Dec (Mon-Sat) 10:00-6:00
    (Sun) 12:30-5:30

Tours:
June-Sept 2:00

Directions:
QEW exit Niagara St., go north, then east on Lakeshore Rd. Winery 7.2 km between Firelines 5 & 6.

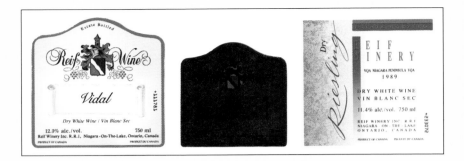

Reif Estate Winery

R eif Estate Winery is situated on the Niagara Parkway, the romantic road with vibrant foliage along the meandering Niagara River. This 35-kilometre (22-mile) drive, one of the loveliest scenic drives in Niagara, prepares you for an enjoyable tour of a winery with Germanic charm and Old World appeal.

Although relatively new, Reif's lineage dates back over 200 years to Germany, where the Reifs grew European viniferas and produced varietal wines at the family-operated winery, Wein Reif GmbH.

In 1977 Ewald Reif (Wein Reif's 12th-generation winemaker) immigrated to Canada and purchased a 34-hectare (83-acre) vineyard located on the Niagara Parkway. He replanted his labrusca and hybrid vineyard to the more desirable varietals of Chardonnay, Kerner, Gewürztraminer, Riesling and Gamay. Five years later Ewald, with his brother Guenther and nephew Klaus, bought the neighbouring 20-hectare (50-acre) vineyard and opened Reif Winery.

Each year their 54-hectare (133-acre) vineyard produces 450 metric tons (500 tons) of premium European vinifera and French-hybrid grapes. Of this

Winemaker Klaus W. Reif with his wife, Sabina Muench

Reif's award-winning wines

amount, Reif keeps 225 metric tons (250 tons) and sells the remaining 225 metric tons to other local wineries.

Klaus W. Reif, Reif's president and winemaker, is a graduate of the world-famous winemaking school Geisenheim University in Germany. Like his predecessors, his winemaking style is traditional.

"I use 100 percent of a specified grape in each of my varietals," says Klaus. "My whites are aged in century-old oak barrels. This method allows my wines to breathe and, in turn, brings out their subtle flavours."

To give his Medium and Late Harvest Riesling a more characteristic flavour, Klaus sweetens these wines with natural grape juice. His Eiswein (Icewine), made from frozen Vidal grapes harvested in winter, has won several international awards, including gold and silver medals at the InterVin International Wine Competition.

Reif makes 21 varietals, and all of these wines are made according to VQA production standards. The winery will soon include an expanded retail boutique, restaurant, outside barbecue, touring and tasting facility, and education centre.

Reif Estate Winery
RR#1, Niagara Parkway
Niagara-on-the-Lake, Ont. L0S 1J0
(416) 468-7738
Fax (416) 468-5878

Wine Boutique:
April-Oct (Daily) 10:00-6:00
Nov-Mar (Daily) 10:00-5:00

Tours:
By appointment

Directions:
QEW exit #38A, go north on Hwy 55 to Niagara-on-the-Lake. Turn east on East-West Line, then south on Niagara Parkway. Winery between Line 2 & 3.

Inniskillin Wines

There is more to Inniskillin Wines than its stucco facade and quaint decor. There is the knowledgeable Debi Pratt, who conducts one of the most informative and fun-filled tours on the peninsula. And then there are co-owners president Donald Ziraldo and winemaker Karl Kaiser, whose distinctive talents and focused energies have created the magic of Inniskillin.

Ziraldo and Kaiser are the creative forces behind this successful winery. After graduating from the University of Guelph in 1971 with a degree in Agriculture, Ziraldo took charge of the family business, Ziraldo Farms & Nurseries. It was here that he met Kaiser, an Austrian whose winemaking experience began at age 13 in the vineyards of a Cistercian monastery. Through a mutual love of wine, a friendship developed, one that would evolve into a partnership.

In the early 1970s General George Kitching, chief commissioner of the LCBO, encouraged Kaiser and Ziraldo to seek a license in the new category of cottage wineries. On July 31, 1975, they received the first wine license issued in Ontario since 1929.

Ziraldo and Kaiser set up the winery in a small fruit-packing barn located on a site originally owned by Colonel Cooper, a member of the Inniskilling Fusiliers during the War of 1812. In honour of this Irish regiment, they named their new company Inniskillin Wines.

Over the next few years Ziraldo focused his energy on market research, sales and promotion, as well as his crusade to persuade Ontario's wine industry to establish a set of official standards (VQA standards). Kaiser concentrated on producing the wine while working on his master's chemistry degree at Brock University. By the fourth year Inniskillin had sold over 900,000 bottles of wine, and oeniphiles around the world began to notice and appreciate Ontario wines.

Today Inniskillin produces 27 varietal wines that emphasize VQA standards. Some of these varietals have won international awards. For example, Kaiser has won gold and silver medals for his Riesling Reserve, Icewine, Gewürztraminer and Pinot Noir Reserve in such competitions as the InterVin International Wine Competition and the International Wine and Spirit Competition in London, England. He recently won the prestigious

Karl Kaiser and Donald Ziraldo

Grand Prix d'Honneur presented in June 1991 for 1989 Icewine at Vin Expo, Bordeaux, the largest wine trade show in the world. He is able to make these quality wines because he does not have to meet stringent production schedules. He can wait until grapes are at their peak before he harvests. Of all the wines Kaiser makes, his Pinot Noir Reserve, made from 100-percent Ontario grapes, is undoubtedly his pride and joy.

Unlike Cabernet Sauvignon, Pinot Noir is difficult to grow and vinify. Kaiser must work hard to get everything he can out of the berries. During fermentation he manually mixes the juice up to three times per day so that all colour and tannins are extracted from the skins. His Pinot Noir Reserve is aged in French Allier and Nevers oak cooperage for up to nine months.

Through the sheer dedication and hard work of its owners, Inniskillin Wines now exports to the United States, Japan, England, Denmark and France, and enjoys a distinguished international reputation.

Inniskillin Wines	**Tours:**
RR #1, Niagara Parkway	June-Oct (Daily) 10:30 & 2:30
Niagara-on-the-Lake, Ont. L0S 1J0	Nov-May (Sat & Sun) 2:30
(416) 468-3554	
Fax (416) 468-5355	**Directions:**
	QEW exit Queenston cut-off, go
Wine Boutique:	east on Hwy 405, then north on
Nov-April (Sun-Mon) 10:00-5:00	Niagara Parkway, then west on
May-Oct (Sun-Mon) 10:00-6:00	Line 3.

Marynissen Estates

(Niagara-on-the-Lake)

M arynissen Estates is located in Niagara-on-the-Lake. Its owner and vintner, John Marynissen, has been a prize-winning amateur wine-maker and now specializes in growing vinifera varieties and making red wines, such as a Cabernet Sauvignon, a Cabernet-Merlot blend and a Merlot Barrel Select. He also makes white wines and has won several awards for some of these products. His 1987 Riesling, for example, won the Best Estate Bottled Wine Award at the American Wine Society competition in 1989 in Philadelphia, and his 1989 Chardonnay won Best of Show Award at the American Wine Society competition in Pittsburgh.

Winemaker John Marynissen

John Marynissen and family

A vineyard in winter

Marynissen Estates
RR #6, Concession #1
Niagara-on-the-Lake, Ont. L0S 1J0
(416) 468-7270
Fax (416) 468-5784

Wine Boutique: Daily 10:00-6:00

Tours: By appointment

Directions: QEW exit #32B
(Queenston cut-off), go east on
405, then north on Niagara River
Parkway. West to Line 3 and south
on Concession 1. Winery between
Line 3 and Larkin Rd.

Brights Wines

Every year more than 70,000 people tour Brights Wines, Canada's oldest and largest winery. With operations in eight provinces, Brights holds nearly a third of the domestic wine market in Canada and produces over 34 million litres (8.8 million gallons) of wine each year.

The original winery, Niagara Falls Wine Co., was founded in 1874 by merchants Thomas G. Bright and Francis Sherriff. In 1890 the winery was relocated to Niagara Falls in order that Bright and Sherriff could be closer to the vineyards. In 1908 Thomas Bright passed away, leaving his eldest son, William, in charge of the company. William bought out Sherriff's shares in 1911 and changed the company name to T.G. Bright & Company Limited, in honour of his father. He ran the company until June 1933, at which time he sold to Harry C. Hatch.

Barrel aging room at Brights

To keep up with Canada's changing tastes toward table wines Hatch sent his research director, Adhemar de Chaunac, on an expedition to collect vine clippings from different wine regions around the world. De Chaunac returned with several dozen French hybrid varieties and 100 different vinifera varieties. He experimented with these vines, crossing Ontario's labruscas with the hybrids and viniferas. In 1966 Brights became the first winery to produce Ontario wines made from hybrid and vinifera varieties. They also introduced the first Chardonnay and Pinot champagne to the Canadian wine market.

Brights continues to be a leader in vinicultural and viticultural research in Canada, and to date, they have invested more than $6 million in the process.

While most winemaking styles are cultural, traditional or personal, Brights considers their winemaking style North American. "We concentrate on meeting the constant and changing demands of the North American people," says James Berry, vice-president of Brights Wines. "We believe in giving our customers what they want."

In response to their customers' latest demand for more blended wines, Brights Wines created a sister company called Sawmill Creek. This line consists of 11 wines that combine Ontario wines with varietals from Chile, Yugoslavia, Washington State, Bordeaux and Beaujolais.

Brights Wines	**Tours:**
4887 Dorchester Rd.	May-Oct (Daily) 10:30 & 2:00 & 3:30
Niagara Falls, Ont. L2E 6V4	Nov-April (Mon-Fri) 2:00
(416) 358-7141 or 1-800-563-WINE	(Sat & Sun) 2:00 & 3:30
Fax (416) 358-7750	(Group tours available on request)
Wine Boutique: Mon-Fri 9:30-10:00	**Directions:** QEW exit Dorchester
Sat 9:30-6:00	Rd., go north. Winery on corner
Sun 12:00-5:00	of Dorchester & Morrison Rd.

Touring Lake Erie North Shore and Pelee Island

Wine. . .is a great increaser of the vital spirits: it very greatly comforteth
a weak stomach, helpeth concoction, distribution and nutrition,
mightily strengtheneth the natural heat, openeth obstruction,
discusseth windiness, taketh away the sadness
and other hurt of melancholy.
Tobias Venner, *Via recta*, 1620

The scenic drive along Highways 3 and 18 will take you through historic villages, modern towns and some of the most beautiful countryside in Ontario. This route will also take you to London Winery near Blenheim, Pelee Island Winery in Kingsville, and Colio Wines in Harrow.

Blenheim's history dates back to the War of 1812, when many United Empire Loyalists settled here after fleeing the United States. The population began to increase as landed immigrants chose "The Golden Acres" as their

new home. These settlers cleared the timbered land to make room for their farms and village. Today Blenheim's attractions include Lake Erie and Rondeau Bay, Gravel Ridge and London Winery.

Kingsville, also known as "The Port of Appeal," is Canada's southernmost town and one of the oldest communities in Essex County. It was named after Colonel James King, and for many years it served as a supply centre and mill town for this agricultural region. Today Kingsville is known as a resort town, tourist destination and an important stop on the migration path of the Canada goose. You will find many tourist attractions, such as the Colasanti Tropical Gardens and Petting Farm, the Jack Miner Bird Sanctuary, and Pelee Island Winery.

Once back on Highway 18, proceed to the town of Harrow. It is said that this community was named after a famous English educational institution. In the 1800s Harrow was an isolated community with a population of only 150. With the construction of a railway in 1880 and the Harrow Research Station in 1909, Harrow's industry and population began to grow. Its close proximity to Lake Erie and favourable climate make Harrow a popular resort area. There are many activities to be found here, such as boating, fishing and shopping.

London Winery

L ondon Winery was established in 1925 by the Knowles family. By 1927 their products were on sale in liquor stores across Ontario. Since that time London Winery has remained a leader in the Canadian wine industry. They were the first to use the revolutionary Flor process in sherry-making, a method developed by Ralph Crowther at the Vineland Horticultural Research Station. They also introduced the first commercial wine decanter with a hollow glass stopper. And in 1965 the company made another noteworthy decision when they took over the Strawa Honey Company and began to produce "Ancient Mead," an alcoholic drink made from fermented honey.

Jim Patience, Peter Knowles and Judy King are the talented winemakers at London Wines. They produce a full range of products, such as sherry, port, vermouth, table wines, sparkling wines, honey wines and fruit wines.

The winery owns a 24-hectare (60-acre) vineyard at Cedar Springs, which is planted to vinifera and hybrid grape varieties. However, grapes are also purchased from other growers on the Niagara Peninsula and foreign wines are brought into Canada for blending.

Although the winery is located in London, they have a retail outlet between Blenheim and Cedar Springs.

The London Winery touring facility

London Wines	**Tours:**
RR #1	May-Sept (Daily) 2:00
Blenheim, Ont. N0P 1A0	Oct-April (Mon-Sat) 2:00
(519) 676-8008	
	Directions:
Wine Boutique:	401 exit Hwy 40 west to Blenheim,
May-Sept (Mon-Sat) 10:00-6:00	then west on Talbot St. (Hwy 3).
(Sun) 12:00-5:00	Winery 4.8 km outside Blenheim.

Colio Wines

The town of Harrow is known as a prosperous farming community, a growing resort area, and the home of Colio Wines.

Founded in 1980, Colio Wines is Ontario's largest boutique winery, producing over 1.6 million litres (416,000 gallons) of wine each year. They purchase approximately 1,300 metric tons (1,430 tons) of grapes from six vineyards in Essex County. However, they recently purchased a 40-hectare (100-acre) vineyard planted primarily with vinifera varieties. Look for estate-bottled products in the future. With the exception of three semi-dry wines, all of Colio's products are dry and fruity.

"I make all my wines in a traditional Italian style," says Carlo Negri, master winemaker at Colio. "Not all my premium wines are aged in wood. My 1990 Pinot Blanc, for instance, is not aged in oak because I do not want a wood taste to interfere or cover its naturally delicate aroma."

To achieve a wine of quality, Negri filters the fresh grape juice, extracting all its impurities before fermentation. This is important if the grapes have been damaged by disease or atmospheric agents. Filtering out the bacteria prevents wild yeasts and germs from growing in the fermenting wine. Negri

Colio Wines' tasting room

Winemaker Carlo Negri

uses a rotary drum vacuum filter specifically designed for filtration of the freshly pressed grape juice. As a result he is able to utilize 100 percent of the juice, and his wines are fruity with a fresh, clean taste.

Negri's Winemaker's Reserve recently brought home a silver medal from the 1991 Toronto Wine & Cheese Show. This full-bodied dry red wine is a blend of Marechal Foch and Cabernet Sauvignon. Its ruby-red colour and predominant Cabernet nose make it a perfect wine to accompany red meat and game.

Colio Wines
Colio Drive
P.O. Box 372
Harrow, Ont. N0R 1G0
(519) 738-2241
Fax (519) 738-3070

Wine Boutique:
Mon-Sat 10:00-5:00

Tours:
Wed 1:00
Sat (hourly from 12:00 till 4:00)

Directions:
401 to Walker Rd. south. In
Harrow, Walker turns into Queen
St. Continue on Queen, then east
on Colio Dr.

Pelee Island Winery

The shores of Lake Erie are home to one of Ontario's most picturesque wineries, Pelee Island Winery and Vineyards Inc. The winery's new Wine Pavilion is situated on Pelee Island and is the Disneyland of Ontario's wine world.

Your tour begins with a peaceful ride across Lake Erie aboard the Pelee Island or Upper Canada ferry. Both ferries service the towns of Leamington and Kingsville, Ontario, and Sandusky, Ohio. Upon reaching the island, a tram will take you to the Pavilion, where your tour will continue with an audio-visual show explaining Pelee Island's history, geology, geography, flora, fauna, and recreational potential. You will also see a presentation on viticulture and viniculture, followed by a creative moment at the computer terminals, where you can design your own wine label.

Lunch is available at the Pavilion. You can munch on cold cuts and cheese or purchase a steak or hamburger and barbecue it yourself outside on the gas barbecues. You can actually eat inside refurbished 8,000-litre (2,080-gallon) wine barrels, complete with tables and benches!

Winemaker Walter Schmoranz

Old wine press at Pelee Island Winery

No winery tour would be complete without a chance to taste some of the winemaker's creations. In the cellar barrel room you may sample a few of winemaker Walter Schmoranz's 18 products.

"I try to make all my wines unique and distinct," says Schmoranz. "For instance, one of my Chardonnays is crisp and light with a higher acidity, while the other is toasty, more fruity, has a higher alcohol content and goes through a malolactic fermentation."

Leaving the winery without one of Schmoranz's red wines would be like leaving home without your shoes. His Fenian's Cuvée has been recognized as excellent at such important competitions as the Eastern International Wine Competition and the InterVin International Wine Competition. His Pinot Noir is complex, with characteristic strawberry and cherry flavours.

In making his Pinot Noir, Schmoranz extracts the juice from the skins after four or ten days. The balance of the fermentation and aging is done in French oak barrels.

Be sure to bring the whole family on your tour of Pelee Island. The children will enjoy themselves at Canada's southernmost petting zoo and at the supervised playground adjacent to the pavilion.

Pelee Island Winery
455 Hwy 18 East
Kingsville, Ont. N9Y 2K5
(519) 733-6551
Fax (519) 733-6553

Wine Boutique:
May-Sept (Daily) 10:00-7:00
Weekends after Labour Day

Tours:
May-Nov (Daily) 12:00 &
2:00 & 4:00

Directions:
401 exit Hwy 77 north, then west
on Hwy 18. Winery 11 km outside
Leamington.

Wineries with Informal Touring Facilities

Wine rejoices the heart of man, and joy is the mother of all virtue.
J.W. Goethe, *Götz von Berlichingen,* 1773

Cartier Wines & Beverages

THIS COMPANY has had several names (including Stamford Park Wine Company Ltd. and Canadian Wineries), having survived a long history of growth and change. Its most memorable name, however, is Chateau-Gai Wines Limited.

In 1980 Chateau-Gai, along with Stoneycroft and Casabello, consolidated as Ridout Wines Ltd., a division of John Labatt Ltd. Although the company bore a new name, the wines kept their original labels.

Under the direction of Ridout Wines Ltd., Chateau-Gai went on to claim more than 18 percent of Canada's estimated $250-million wine market by producing wines such as Alpenweiss, L'Ambiance and Capistro.

The greatest change in Ridout's history took place on July 5, 1989, when the management team acquired the company. Thus, Ridout Wines Ltd. became Cartier Wines & Beverages, and a new corporate identity was established, that of a modern, approachable, innovative winery committed to excellence and service.

For over a hundred years this wine company has been an innovator in the Canadian wine industry. Under the direction of the late Dr. Alex G. Sampson, Chateau-Gai purchased the Canadian rights for the *methode Charmat*, a French technique for making sparkling wines. The bag-in-box and Canada Cooler were also invented by Chateau-Gai, as was Capistro, the first "light" wine to be sold in Canada.

For 17 years Mira Ananicz has been the artist behind the scene. She is the only woman in Ontario to hold the position of chief winemaker. Among her many great innovations, she is most proud of her 1982 Chardonnay and 1982 Chancellor, two varietals that were selected in a blind tasting at the Office of Protocol. These wines were served to the Queen on her visit to Canada in 1982. "For the blind tasting, each of Canada's wineries was asked to present one white and one red wine," explains Mira. "It was an honour for me that my wines were chosen in both categories."

In addressing market demand, Cartier has produced six varietals, all of which are VQA listed. Cartier is also creating beverages with reduced to zero alcohol levels (low-alcohol wines and coolers), juice coolers, carbonated juices, dairy-based refreshment beverages, and draft beverages.

Cartier Wines & Beverages
2625 Stanley Avenue
Niagara Falls, Ontario
L2E 6T8
(416) 354-1631
Fax (416) 354-0161

Wine Boutique Hours
Monday through Friday
9:00 - 4:30
No touring facilities

Winemaker Mira Ananicz of Cartier Wines

Lakeview Cellars

LAKEVIEW CELLARS Estate Winery Limited is located on the bench of the escarpment in Vineland. The winery was started by Ed and Lorraine Gurinskas, and construction of a new building is now under way. It will house the new winery, tasting room and retail outlet. Grand-opening celebrations are scheduled for summer 1992.

Winemaker Ed Gurinskas has been making wine since the early 1960s. He is an acclaimed amateur winemaker with many medals and awards to his credit. The most treasured of his wines now available is a 1990 Vidal Icewine. Ed has also released his 1990 Cabernet Sauvignon, a dry red wine. To be released this spring are the winery's whites: Riesling (0), Welschriesling (1), Estate Vidal (2), Estate Chardonnay (0) and a white house wine. Several red wines will be released at a later date.

Lakeview Cellars
R.R. #1
4037 Cherry Avenue
Vineland, Ontario
L0R 2C0
(416) 562-5685

Joseph Barkovic, brix grader for the Ontario
Ministry of Agriculture

Culotta Wines Limited
(Oakville)

IN 1984 Culotta produced approximately 2,000 cases of Kimberly White Wine and Christopher Red Wine. Production increased rapidly over the next seven years, and by the end of 1990 they had sold over 30,000 cases of six blended whites, three blended reds and a limited edition of Gewürztraminer and Sauvignon Blanc. Winemaker Robert Claremont also produces blends that combine wines from Ontario, Chile and California. Culotta Wines Ltd. offers tours by appointment only.

Culotta Wines Limited
1185 North Service Road East
Oakville, Ontario
(416) 844-7912
Fax (416) 844-2228

D'Angelo Vineyards
(Amherstburg)

THE NEWEST of the new Windsor wineries is located on Sal D'Angelo's farm. This prize-winning amateur has gone commercial, producing "only the noble varietals" such as Riesling, Chardonnay, Gamay, Merlot, Cabernet-Sauvignon and Pinot Blanc. Call ahead for directions.

D'Angelo Vineyards
R.R. #4, 5141 5th Concession
P.O. Box 208
Amherstburg, Ontario N9V 2Y9
(519) 736-7959

De Sousa Cellars
(Beamsville)

DE SOUSA CELLARS was established in 1987 by John and Mary De Sousa. Winemaker Dieter Guttler produces his Dois Amigos red and white table wines in a traditional Portuguese style. Both wines are made from 100-percent Ontario grapes grown on De Sousa's 27-hectare (66-acre) vineyard. His white wine is a blend of Riesling, Vidal and Chardonnay, while his red wine combines de Chaunac, Pinot Noir and Marechal Foch. Soon the winery will include a retail store and a museum featuring the history of Portuguese wines. Call ahead for tour information.

De Sousa Cellars
3753 Quarry Road
Beamsville, Ontario
(416) 362-3068

Jordan Valley looking south

Row on row of vines ready for harvest

Quai Du Vin Estate Winery Ltd.
(St. Thomas)

AS AN AMATEUR winemaker, Roberto Quai won 1st Place and Best White Wine of Show for the 1988 Riesling he presented at the Amateur Winemakers of Ontario contest. Quai operates a farm winery called Quai Du Vin Estate Winery. Each year his company produces over 38,000 litres (10,000 gallons) of white varietal wines such as Chardonnay, Vidal and Riesling, as well as a few reds. Call ahead for a personal tour.

Quai Du Vin Estate Winery Ltd.
R.R. #5
St. Thomas, Ontario
N5P 3S9
(519) 775-2216

Vinoteca
(Woodbridge)

ALL THE WINES at Vinoteca are made from Ontario grapes grown on the Niagara Peninsula. Winemaker Giovanni Follegot makes a few white wines (Chardonnay, Riesling and a blend called Albino) but concentrates mainly on his red wines. His Cabernet Sauvignon, Baco Noir and Pinot Noir are all made in a traditional Italian style; they are produced in stainless steel, which brings out their fruit flavours and natural sweetness. Vinoteca offers tours by appointment only.

Vinoteca
61 Caster Avenue
Woodbridge, Ontario
L4L 5Z2
(416) 856-5700

Southbrook Farms
(Maple)

SOUTHBROOK is the newest of Ontario's wineries, housed in an old dairy barn. Chief winemaker Bill Redelmeir uses mostly Niagara grapes to produce his wines, which include a light and heavy Chardonnay, dry and off-dry Riesling, and Pinot Noir Vin Gris.

Southbrook Farms
1061 Major Mackenzie Drive
Maple, Ontario
L0J 1E0
(416) 832-2548

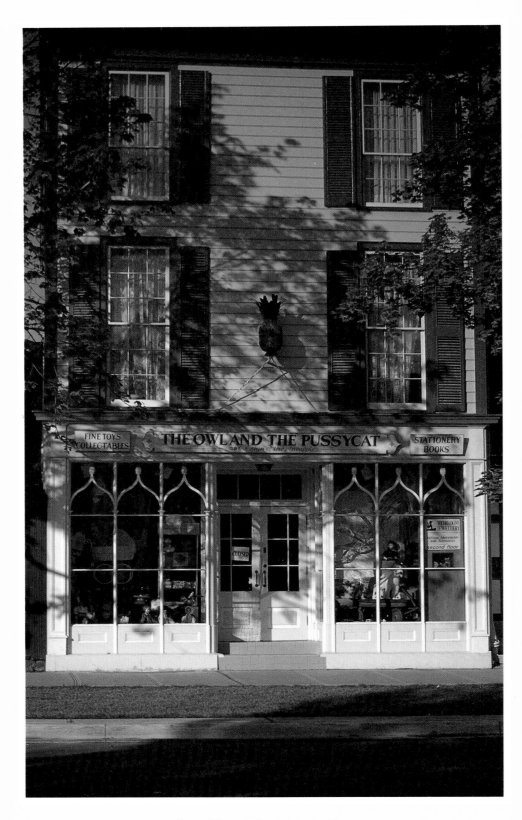

One of the area's many attractions

Accommodations, Dining and Diversions

Drink a glass of wine after your soup, and you steal a ruble from the doctor. Russian proverb

ACCOMMODATIONS

MANY HOTELS and motels are scattered throughout Ontario's wine regions, and finding one to suit your needs, pleasures and price range will not be difficult. However, a Bed & Breakfast home (B&B) will offer you more than just reasonably priced accommodation. A B&B will allow you to capture the true spirit and character of the town you are visiting.

Although privately run, many B&Bs are members of local organizations or affiliated with their area Chamber of Commerce. The agencies listed below offer a referral service for B&Bs in their area:

Niagara-on-the-Lake Chamber of Commerce
P.O. Box 1043
153 King Street
Niagara-on-the-Lake, Ontario
L0S 1J0
(416) 468-4263

Niagara Falls Chamber of Commerce
4394 Queen Street
Niagara Falls, Ontario
L2E 2L3
(416) 374-3666

Niagara Falls Visitor and Convention Bureau
5433 Victoria Avenue
Niagara Falls, Ontario
L2G 3L1
(416) 356-6061

St. Catharines Bed & Breakfast Association
28 Cartier Drive
St. Catharines, Ontario
L2M 2E7
(416) 937-2422

Leamington District Chamber of Commerce
35 Mill Street West
Leamington, Ontario
N8H 1S7
(519) 326-2721

Point Pelee Bed & Breakfast Association (Referral Service)
115 Erie Street South
Leamington, Ontario
N8H 3B5
(519) 326-7169

Pelee Island Bed & Breakfast Association
General Delivery
Pelee Island, Ontario
N0R 1M0
(519) 724-2068

DINING

THE BEST WAY to appreciate Ontario wines is to enjoy them with your meals. What better way to do this than to dine in the restaurants situated in the heart of Ontario's wine regions? The restaurants listed below offer a variety of cuisines and a broad selection of Ontario wines. Call ahead for hours of business and reservation requirements.

ST. CATHARINES
Albert's
61 Lakeport Rd.
(416) 646-5000

Astina's Restaurant
80 King Street
Casual/Fine Dining
(416) 682-4444

Auberge Suisse
15 Lyman Street
European/French Cuisine
(416) 684-8354

The Cellar Bench
81 James Street
(416) 641-1922

Holiday Inn
Oregano's Ristorante
Corner of Lake & QEW Hwy
Canadian Cuisine
(416) 934-2561

The Old Bank Restaurant
101 St. Paul Street
(Queen & St. Paul)
Casual/Fine Dining
(416) 685-6637

The Port Mansion
12 Lakeport Road
(Old Port Dalhousie)
Casual/Fine Dining
(416) 934-0575

*Fishing and boating on
the Niagara River*

Antiquing in Niagara

Wellington Court Cafe
11 Wellington Street
(on Wellington between
Duke & Church)
Casual/Eclectic Cuisine
(416) 682-5518

NIAGARA-ON-THE-LAKE

The Buttery Theatre Restaurant
19 Queen Street
English and Colonial Luncheons
Henry VIII Feasts
(416) 468-2564

Fans Court
135 Queen Street
Family Dining
(416) 468-4511

Prince of Wales, Niagara-on-the-Lake

Gate House Hotel
Giardino's Restaurant
142 Queen Street
Italian
(416) 468-3263

Luis House
245 King Street
(King & Johnson)
Family Dining
(416) 468-4038

The Oban Inn
160 Front Street
(Front & Gate)
Casual/Fine Dining
(416) 468-2165

Pillar & Post Inn
(Corner of King & John)
Canadian Cuisine
(416) 468-2123

Prince of Wales Hotel
The Royals Dining Room
8 Picton Street
Continental Cuisine
(416) 468-3246

Niagara Falls

Queen's Landing Inn Dining Room
(Corner of Byron & Melville)
Continental Cuisine
(416) 468-2195

NIAGARA FALLS

Queenston Heights Restaurant
Queenston Heights Park
Canadian Cuisine
(416) 262-4274

Table Rock
(on Niagara Parkway near the
brink of Horseshoe Falls)
Canadian
(416) 354-3631

Victoria Park
Niagara Parkway
(Bottom of Murray Hill
opposite the American Falls)
Continental
(416) 356-2217

The Brock Hotel
Rainbow Room
5685 Falls Avenue
Fine Dining
(416) 374-4444

The Foxhead
Penthouse Restaurant
5685 Falls Avenue
Buffet Style
(416) 374-4444

Pardon My Garden Cafe
5703 Ferry Street
Casual/Fine Dining
(416) 357-3505

Ramada
Mulberry Room
6455 Buchanan
Buffet Style Dining
(416) 357-5200, Ext. 6240

Rolf's Continental Dining
3840 Main Street
French/Continental with German
Influence
(416) 295-3472

Skylon Tower
Revolving Dining Room
5200 Robinston Street
Niagara's Tallest Tower
(416) 356-2651

WELLAND

Rinderlin's Dining Rooms
24 Burgar Street
Fine Dining
(416) 735-4411

**PELEE ISLAND &
LAKE ERIE NORTH SHORE**

Danilo's
10672 County Road 42
Maidstone, Ontario
Italian
(519) 979-3017

Essex House
19 Laird Avenue
Essex, Ontario
Home cooked Canadian
(519) 776-7713

L'Auberge de la Bastille
149 Chatham Street West
Windsor, Ontario
French/Canadian
(519) 256-2555

Rinderlin's Dining Rooms, Welland

The Grape & Wine Festival

Louie Linquini's
139 Ouellette Avenue
Windsor, Ontario
Italian
(519) 252-6969

Red Sail
3838 Walker Road
Windsor, Ontario
Chinese / Canadian
(519) 969-6921

TBQ's Other Place
3067 Dougal Road
Windsor, Ontario
International
(519) 969-6011

WINE & FOOD FESTIVAL AT COLASANTI'S

On the first weekend in June this festival pays tribute to the wineries, restaurants and citizens situated in and around Essex County. Festival events include wine tastings, seminars, contests, entertainment and food from local restaurants.

For more information call
(519) 733-3571
Colasanti's Farms
R.R. #2
Ruthven, Ontario
N9Y 2E5

Contact the individual wineries for details of other events held throughout the year, such as special tastings, wine clubs, gourmet dinners, etc. Also, the Ontario Wine Society hosts several interesting wine events annually: call (416) 890-1309.

1991 Grape Queen, Donna Lailey, rewarded for the quality of her vineyards

DIVERSIONS IN ONTARIO'S WINE COUNTRY

Cuvée

Held the first weekend in March, Cuvée is a celebration of excellence in Ontario winemaking. It is a weekend-long event consisting of a Gala Evening (wine tasting and gourmet fare with musical entertainment), Luncheon (featuring renowned wine speaker), and Cuvée En Route (private wine tastings at wineries throughout the region by reservation only).

For more information call
Grey Gables School
(416) 685-4577
or (416) 685-3707

Hillebrand's Jazz Festival

Held the first weekend in July, this is an outdoor festival of wine, food and live jazz. Bring your own blanket and/or lawn chair.

For more information call
Hillebrand Winery
(416) 468-3201 or (416) 468-7123
Tickets available at any of
Hillebrand's retail stores
throughout Ontario.

Niagara Grape & Wine Festival

Held the last ten days in September, this is a festival at which thousands of visitors take part in the celebration of grape harvest. The festivities include wine gardens, wine tastings, musical performances, contests, arts and crafts, winery tours, parades, and much more.

For more information call
The Niagara Grape & Wine Festival
145 King Street
St. Catharines
(416) 688-0212

A Glossary of Ontario Wine Terms

Acidity — The agreeable sharp taste caused by natural fruit acids. In moderate amount it is a favourable characteristic, and is not to be confused with sourness, dryness, or astringency.

Aging — The process of allowing time to fully blend and develop the character of a wine. The span differs greatly with different wines.

Aroma — The fragrance of fresh fruit directly related to the variety of grape used to make the wine. The aroma of wine will change as the wine ages to its final bouquet.

Astringency — A normal characteristic of some young wines, usually caused by an excess of tannin, lessening with age. It has a puckering effect on the mouth. It is more noticeable with red wines.

Balance — A term of high praise denoting a wine whose sugar content, acidity, and the many odour and taste elements are present in such proportions as to produce a harmonious and pleasant sensation.

Blending — The specialized craft of combining two or more wines to achieve a batch of wine of high standard and uniform quality.

Body — The taste sensation of substance in a wine, which can be related to alcoholic content. Wine may have a heavy body or a light body. This cannot be measured. It is a matter of taste.

Bouquet — The complex of odours given off by a mature wine when it is opened.

Breathing — Wines breathe when they are in contact with the air. A young red wine will benefit from being given at least half an hour to breathe.

Brut — French term designating driest (least sweet) grade of champagne or sparkling wine.

Character — The combination of taste, bouquet and colour in a wine.

Cooperage — The general term used to designate containers in which wines are stored and aged. It includes casks and wooden or stainless steel aging tanks. The term derives from the occupation of cooper, one who makes or repairs wooden containers.

Corked or Corky — A "corked" or "corky" wine is very rare and may occur from a faulty cork. A musty, unpleasant smell and taste will be present.

Decant — To pour wine from one container to another.

Dessert Wines — Wines fortified with alcohol to give them a final high alcoholic content of 14 to 20% alcohol by volume, they can be either sweet or dry e.g., port, sherry.

Dosage — The sweetener added to bottles of sparkling wine or champagne after degorging of sediment accumulated during secondary fermentation in the bottle.

Dry — This much-abused word means nothing more than lacking in sweetness. The degree of dryness is determined by the proportion of total grape sugar converted to alcohol.

Estate-Bottled — These words indicate that the wine was produced and bottled on a property controlled by the winery.

Extra Dry — A contradictory term used on champagne labels meaning somewhat sweet. The degree of sweetness varies.

Fermentation — A process whereby yeasts interact with sugars to produce alcohol and carbon dioxide. It is through such a process that grape juice is transformed into wine.

Fining — A traditional process of clarification. The fining medium settles to the bottom carrying with it the fine suspended particles.

Flor — The variety of yeast giving the character peculiar to dry sherries.

Flowery — A term denoting the fragrance of blossoms in a wine's bouquet or aroma.

Fortified Wine — Wine such as sherry, port, and muscatel to which alcohol has been added, usually in the form of brandy or grape spirit to increase their alcoholic content. This is a world-wide practice.

Foxiness — The pronounced aroma characteristic of many native labrusca grapes.

Frappé — The notation *Servir frappé* is sometimes found on white wine labelling; it means — Serve iced or chilled.

Fruity — Term applied to a fine young wine which has the aroma and flavour of fresh fruit.

Full — Pleasingly strong in flavour, bouquet, or taste.

Generic — A wine type having certain characteristics not related to its actual origin. Ontario wines labelled Burgundy or Sauterne are using the generic appellation. See Varietal.

Green — Term applied to young wine of excessive acidity.

Hard — Wine taster's term for a wine with excessive tannin. Not necessarily a fault in a young wine, where it may indicate a long maturity.

Heavy — Excessive alcohol content without a corresponding balance of flavour.

Labrusca — The principal species of the native American grape, Vitis labrusca, typical examples of which are the Concord, Catawba, and Niagara.

Lees — The sediment deposited in the storage vats before bottling. The lees are left behind by racking.

90

Light — A complimentary term applied to pleasant refreshing wines; the opposite of full-bodied.

Maturity — A state reached by wine through aging.

Mousseux — A French word, on a wine label, that indicates a sparkling wine.

Must — The grape juice before it is fermented.

Musty — Unpleasant "mousy" odour and flavour, similar to moldy, usually due to unclean cellar.

Nose — Professional winetaster term describing quality of bouquet.

Oxidation — Exposure of wine to air, resulting in deterioration over a long period of time.

Pétillant — Lightly sparkling or crackling wine.

Press — A machine which, by applying direct pressure, forces the juice from the grapes. There are many types of presses, ranging from the ancient hand-operated wooden press to sophisticated hydraulic machines made of stainless steel.

Racking — The process whereby clear wine is drawn off its lees and sediment, and transformed from one storage container to another.

Riddling — In champagne-making, the process of working the sediment into the neck of the bottle during the second fermentation. Traditionally a hand operation, it is now being done mechanically in many wineries.

Rotundifolia — A species of native American grapes having a muscadine or muscat flavour.

Rounded — A complimentary term for a wine whose qualities, while not necessarily individually great are in balance.

Sec — French word for dry. Secco, in Italian, is used similarly.

Sediment — The harmless solid matter thrown by wine during fermentation and aging. It is more pronounced and abundant in red wines than in whites. In the aging process it sometimes forms a crust on the wall of the bottle. Wines with heavy sedimentation must be decanted before serving.

Sekt — Generic type name of German sparkling wines.

Soft — Term describing the pleasant smoothness of wines of low astringency. Not related to sweetness.

Sour — A disagreeable taste sensation, acid and vinegary, indicating a spoiled, undrinkable wine. Not to be confused with tartness, astringency, or dryness.

Spicy — A term used to describe the taste of some wines although no spices have in fact been added to them.

Still Wine — A non-effervescent wine in which the carbon dioxide gas, formed during fermentation, has all escaped. The opposite of sparkling wine.

Table Wines — A wine with a maximum of 14% alcohol by volume. It may be red, white or rosé.

Tart — The sharp, astringent taste of fruit acid, like the taste of a McIntosh apple. When present in a moderate degree, tartness lends a pleasant freshness to a wine.

Tawny — The brownish-red colour acquired by some red wines in aging. The characteristic colour of Tawny Port.

Tannin — An astringent acid found to some degree in all wine, but more in red than white. The proper degree of tannic acid is essential to aged, high quality red wines; an excess can ruin any wine.

Varietal — The wine name taken from the grape variety used to make it. The following are some varietal names: Delaware, Chardonnay, Riesling, Maréchal Foch, de Chaunac, etc. See Generic.

Vinifera — The most important of the 32 species of vines making up the genus Vitis in the botanical classification. Vitis vinifera is the species of grape from which all the wines of Europe are made. It is being successfully introduced into Ontario.

Vinification — This broad term covers the whole process of turning grapes into wine, except for the vineyard operations. It includes fermentation, clarification, and aging.

Vintage — The harvesting, crushing, and fermentation of grapes into wine. This term is also applied to the crop of grapes or the wine of one season.

Vintage Wine — A wine labelled with the year in which most of the grapes from which it was made were harvested and made into wine. (In Ontario at least 85% must be from the year of harvest.) When supported by other information, it usually implies a better quality than its non-vintage counterpart.

Vintner — This broad term, once applied only to wholesale wine merchants, now includes wine growers, wine makers, wine blenders, etc.

Viticulture — The cultivation of the vine, also the science of grape production.

Woody — Term describing the characteristic odour of wine aged in wooden vats and barrels for an extended period. The odour is like that of wet wood.

Yeast — A natural bloom found in grapes, whose fermentive qualities cause sugar to break down into alcohol.

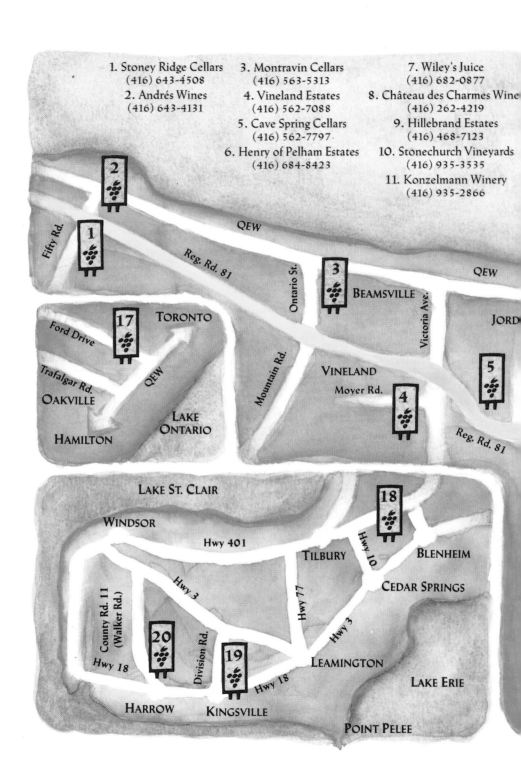

1. Stoney Ridge Cellars
   (416) 643-4508
2. Andrés Wines
   (416) 643-4131
3. Montravin Cellars
   (416) 563-5313
4. Vineland Estates
   (416) 562-7088
5. Cave Spring Cellars
   (416) 562-7797
6. Henry of Pelham Estates
   (416) 684-8423
7. Wiley's Juice
   (416) 682-0877
8. Château des Charmes Wine
   (416) 262-4219
9. Hillebrand Estates
   (416) 468-7123
10. Stonechurch Vineyards
    (416) 935-3535
11. Konzelmann Winery
    (416) 935-2866

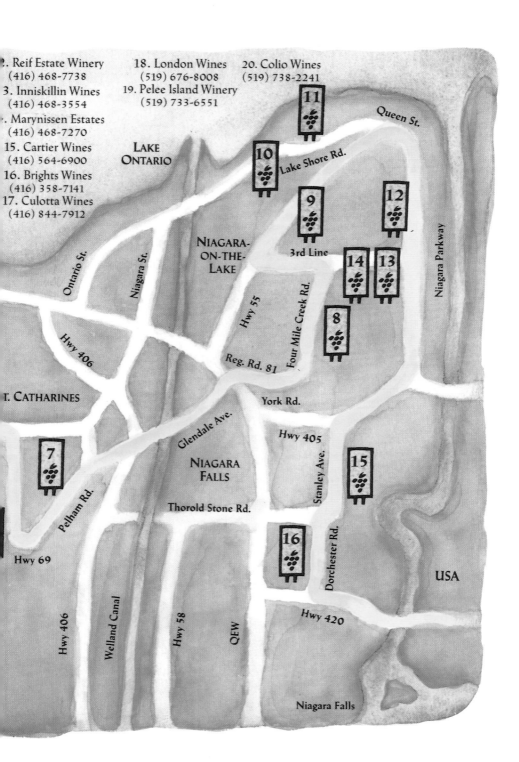

2. Reif Estate Winery
   (416) 468-7738
3. Inniskillin Wines
   (416) 468-3554
. Marynissen Estates
   (416) 468-7270
15. Cartier Wines
   (416) 564-6900
16. Brights Wines
   (416) 358-7141
17. Culotta Wines
   (416) 844-7912

18. London Wines
   (519) 676-8008
19. Pelee Island Winery
   (519) 733-6551

20. Colio Wines
   (519) 738-2241

LAKE ONTARIO

NIAGARA-ON-THE-LAKE

Queen St.

Lake Shore Rd.

3rd Line

Niagara Parkway

Four Mile Creek Rd.

Hwy 55

Reg. Rd. 81

York Rd.

Glendale Ave.

Hwy 405

Stanley Ave.

NIAGARA FALLS

Thorold Stone Rd.

Dorchester Rd.

Ontario St.

Niagara St.

Hwy 406

T. CATHARINES

Pelham Rd.

Hwy 69

Welland Canal

Hwy 58

QEW

Hwy 420

Hwy 406

USA

Niagara Falls

Bibliography

Alec Gold. *Wines and Spirits of the World*. Virtue & Company Ltd., London, 1968.

Aspler, Tony. *Vintage Canada*. Prentice-Hall, Scarborough, Ontario, 1983.

Broadbent, Michael. *The Simon & Schuster Pocket Guide to Wine Tasting*. Simon & Schuster, Toronto, 1979.

Hardy, Thomas, K. *North American Vineyards*. Grape Vision Pty. Ltd., Australia, 1988.

Jackson, David, and Schuster, Danny. *The Production of Grapes and Wines in Cool Climates*. Butterworth Horticultural Books, Wellington, New Zealand, 1981.

Johnson, Hugh. *The World Atlas of Wine*. Simon and Schuster, Toronto, 1985.

Lamb, Richard & Mittelberger, Ernst G. *In Celebration of Wine and Life*. Drake Publishers Inc., New York, 1974.

Peynaud, Emile. *Knowing and Making Wine*. John Wiley and Sons, Toronto, 1984.

Pieroth, Kuno F. *The Great German Wine Book*. Sterling Publishing Co., Inc., New York, 1983.

Postgage, Raymond. *The Plain Man's Guide to Wine*. Michael Joseph, London, 1965.

Rannie, William. *Wines of Ontario: An Industry Coming of Age*. W.F. Rannie, Publisher, Beamsville, Ontario, 1978.

Rowe, Percy. *The Wines of Canada*. McGraw Hill Company of Canada, Toronto, 1970.

Schoonmaker, Frank. *Frank Schoonmaker's Encyclopedia of Wine*. Black, Adam & Charles, London, 1973.

Schreiner, John. *The World of Canadian Wine*. Douglas & McIntyre, Vancouver/Toronto, 1984.

Sharp, Andrew. *Intervin Guide to Award-Winning Wines*. Intervin Marketing Services, Don Mills, Ontario, 1990.

Sharp, Andrew. *Vineland 1000: A Canadian View of Wine*. Andrew Sharp Publications, Toronto, 1977.

Sharp, Andrew. *Winetasters Secrets*. Horizon Publishing/John Wiley Distributors. Toronto/Rexdale, 1981.

Smith, Brian. *Fruit Growing Industry in Canada*. Vanwell Geography Project Series, St. Catharines, 1986.

Spurrier, Steven and Dovas, Michel. *Academie du Vin Wine Course*. Mitchell Beazley Publishers, Great Britain, 1990.

Tovell, Walter M. *The Niagara Escarpment*. The Governors of the University of Toronto, Toronto, 1965.

Wicklund, R.E. *The Soil Survey of Lincoln County*. Soil Research Institute and B.C. Matthews Ontario Agriculture College, Guelph, 1963.

Vandyke Price, Pamela. *Winelovers' Handbook*. Simon & Schuster, New York, 1969.

Index

Photo Credits

About the Authors

Linda Bramble is the author of *Undiscovered Niagara*. She lives in St. Catharines, where she works as a freelance travel and wine writer and is Program Director for the Niagara Institute.

Shari Darling is a freelance writer and the wine editor for *Scene* magazine. She is currently working on a cookbook that marries Canadian wines and food.